Against Landlords

Against Landlords

How to Solve the Housing Crisis

Nick Bano

VERSO

London • New York

First published by Verso 2024
© Nick Bano 2024
Lines from Stephen Spender's *Vienna* reproduced with permission of
Curtis Brown Group Ltd, London, on behalf of the Beneficiaries of the
Estate of Stephen Spender. Copyright © Stephen Spender.

1 3 5 7 9 10 8 6 4 2
Verso
UK: 6 Meard Street, London W1F 0EG
US: 388 Atlantic Avenue, Brooklyn, NY 11217
versobooks.com

Verso is the imprint of New Left Books

ISBN-13: 978-1-80429-387-4
ISBN-13: 978-1-80429-389-8 (US EBK)
ISBN-13: 978-1-80429-388-1 (UK EBK)

British Library Cataloguing in Publication Data
A catalogue record for this book is available from the British Library

Library of Congress Cataloging-in-Publication Data

Names: Bano, Nick, author.
Title: Against landlords : how to solve the housing crisis / Nick Bano.
Description: London ; New York : Verso, 2024. | Includes bibliographical
    references and index.
Identifiers: LCCN 2023043206 (print) | LCCN 2023043207 (ebook) | ISBN
    9781804293874 (hardback) | ISBN 9781804293898 (US ebk) | ISBN
    9781804293881 (UK ebk)
Subjects: LCSH: Housing policy – Great Britain. | Housing – Great Britain.
Classification: LCC HD7333.A3 B26 2024 (print) | LCC HD7333.A3 (ebook) |
    DDC 363.5/5610941 – dc23/eng/20231207
LC record available at https://lccn.loc.gov/2023043206
LC ebook record available at https://lccn.loc.gov/2023043207

Typeset in Fournier by Biblichor Ltd, Scotland
Printed and bound by CPI Group (UK) Ltd, Croydon, CR0 4YY

FSC
www.fsc.org
MIX
Paper | Supporting
responsible forestry
FSC® C171272

'We say Vienna
'Tenements were a fortress built by the workers
'So we killed the workers to save the workers—
'And when those houses were put up we said
'The building materials used by the socialist municipality are of such
    inferior quality that the new working class tenements will soon fall
    to pieces.'
. . .

There were some suffered from the destruction of houses
More than from death of men: they weep for their houses
That endured enormous wounds, a man's abyss.
So the once sun-flaked walls, our elaborated pride,
Were more our life than any man's one life, though proud.
Heroes are instantly replaced: civilization
Wears concrete sides: destroy these walls
With shell-holes, and our children wear their weals.

Stephen Spender, *Vienna* (1934)

Contents

Introduction:
House-Price Capitalism

Poverty is a more fruitful source for house-rent than the [silver] mines of Potosí were for Spain . . . One section of society here demands a tribute from the other for the very right to live on the earth.

Karl Marx, *Capital, Volume III*

Wealth in Britain today appears in the form of an immense collection of house prices. In the seventy years between the 1950s and the Covid-19 pandemic the value of the housing stock in the United Kingdom increased by 500 per cent. In the last of those decades – the ten years between the global financial crisis and the pandemic – the total value rose by £750 million per day. For scale, that is much more than the entire personal wealth of Elizabeth II mysteriously appearing overnight – *every* night – being added to the tally of housing-based wealth. As a result, the national economy went into the pandemic with a housing market that had swollen to four times the size of the combined value of the FTSE 100 companies, and roughly twice the size of the balance sheet of the European Central Bank.

Such an abundance of wealth was excellent news for anyone who had invested in housing, but it has also produced severe social and economic consequences. While all of that wealth was being accrued, we saw a worsening crisis of poverty and living conditions. Housing is something that everyone needs, and virtually everyone has to pay for. The massive rise in the value of housing means that it is now incredibly expensive.

This is a very serious problem: many cannot afford housing at all; others cannot afford the kind of housing that meets their needs in terms of size, location, quality or amenities. We are forced to deny ourselves the things that we need or want in order to accommodate ourselves adequately. In other words, what we have come to call 'the housing crisis' is primarily a crisis of price. Too many people simply cannot afford the kind of housing they would wish to live in.

What explains these extraordinarily high prices? In many respects, Britain is a fairly normal country – its housing statistics are comparable to those of many other high-income countries. And yet the housing crisis here is particularly severe. The number of dwellings per capita in the UK is only just shy of the OECD average. And despite the notorious mass sell-off of council housing under the 'right to buy' scheme since the 1980s, the percentage of socially rented dwellings is still nearly double the EU average.[1]

The crisis of spiralling housing costs cannot be attributed to unique levels of housing scarcity here, nor really to the decimation of council housing – although both of these are pegs on which people often hang their arguments, depending on their political standpoint. In that sense, this book departs from the usual, familiar explanations of the housing crisis. It aims to get to the heart of the question of what is happening in Britain that turns its homes into such hot property.

The overall argument of this book can be summarised thus: the housing crisis is primarily concerned with the cost of housing. Homes have become extremely profitable, and – over the course of several decades – this has made accommodation far too expensive. This was not an accident. Britain has a system of law, regulation and economics that is unusually (if not uniquely) good at allowing rents to rise, because the state guarantees that they will.

These rising rents are translated into rising house prices, because the price of property in land is derived from the yields that the landowner is able, in practice or in principle, to charge in rent. As rents rise, house prices rise as a consequence, and households come under ever-increasing financial hardship in order to accommodate themselves. For as long as the population continues to fork out for these ever-rising costs, house prices will rise, because that is what law and economics encourage them to do.

The housing question has been approached from all sorts of different angles and disciplines. Journalists concentrate on its stories and human consequences; economists tear their hair out over supply and demand; social scientists scrutinise policy measures; and all manner of people describing themselves as geographers write interesting, fashionable texts about urbanism. The housing crisis is multifaceted, and must be viewed through a number of different prisms in order to be understood properly.

This contribution emerges from two fields: first, law; and second, Marx's critique of political economy. The book explores the housing crisis as an interplay between law and economics under capitalism. Modern governments are not really in the business of building homes. Instead, they use the law to pull (or try to pull) the strings of economic actors — and that is the process we need to understand.

Before the 1980s the cost of housing was much lower than it is today. Landlords could not command the extravagant rents that we have come to take for granted. Private rents were capped and regulated by law, and the large-scale provision of council housing had diverted a very large number of would-be consumers away from the private rental market altogether. The cost of securing accommodation was much lower because of those cheaper rents (and, for homeowners, consequentially lower house prices), and because of a system that was generally less hospitable to the profiteering activities of landlords, lenders and speculators.

But in the 1980s the government deliberately and openly set out to change all that. Thatcher's ministers lamented the fact that the private rented sector was in terminal decline, with just 7 per cent (and falling) of households in England having to rent privately. They set out to reverse its fortunes by attracting capital through deregulation. The central charge of this book is that they were very successful in doing so, and that the consequences have been disastrous.

Forty years later, we are now stuck in a situation where both individual household finances and the national economy more broadly are heavily dependent on the wealth generated by housing. This dilemma comes into ever-sharper focus as the population ages and the interests of different generations dominate political choices. The current situation is intolerable: the cost, quality and availability of accommodation have – by common agreement – conspired to produce a crisis that entails immense suffering. We desperately need to interrupt and reverse a system that results in homelessness and squalor, while the lion's share of people's incomes is being spent on housing that is often inadequate. A system that causes so much misery and poverty cannot and must not be tolerated.

On the other hand, housing-based wealth is dangerously central to our national economy. Landlordism alone accounts for twice as many people's livelihoods as the coal industry did at its peak, even before taking into account the millions of owner-occupiers who rely on housing wealth to sustain their day-to-day spending. Ownership remains the dominant form of tenure (62.5 per cent in England and Wales), and homes are very often a substitute for inadequate pensions, a means of funding care in later life, and a bulwark against low pay and an increasingly frayed system of public services. At the national level, rent extraction and land-value speculation are now perhaps the closest thing that Britain has to a national industry, whose failure would have dramatic consequences for the economy more broadly.

For good or ill, we are all affected by the economy. The generation of renters that has lived through the global financial crisis, recession, austerity, Covid and rapid inflation has no need to be told that a faltering national economy can severely impact us all, and will punish the poorest in particular. Therefore, in a certain sense, as well as desperately needing the cost of housing to collapse, we also need the value of housing to be sustained to avoid a cascade of national and personal catastrophes.

We are dependent on our own exploitation in the sense that, as participants in a national economy, we are all reliant on the continued financial success of landlords and homeowners. And yet we delude ourselves into thinking that this tense state of affairs can last for ever. As Kae Tempest put it in their devastatingly moving song *People's Faces*: 'There is too much pretence here; and too much depends on the fragile wages and extortionate rents here.'

Facts and Figures

This book does not provide a close examination of the statistics, or even the personal stories, that make up the current housing crisis. That is partly because there are many first-rate writers and journalists describing the day-to-day developments and the horrors they produce, and partly because the situation deteriorates so quickly that the data tend to become out-of-date as soon as they are printed. In addition, most readers of this book will know exactly how bad the housing crisis is from their own direct experience, rather than through arid statistics. But this is broadly how things stand at the time of writing:

- The sharpest rate of rent increases on record took place in 2022: 20.5 per cent in Manchester, 19.6 per cent in Cardiff, 18 per cent in Edinburgh, 17.6 per cent in Birmingham and 16.1 per cent in London.[2]

- In 2023 the UK had the highest proportion of homeless households in the OECD: it is the only member-state in which the figure exceeds 1 per cent.[3]
- Figures for 2023 showed that 100,000 children were growing up in temporary accommodation. This is insecure short-term housing paid for by local authorities.[4] In England alone, more than three times that number (313,244 children) were having to share beds with family members.[5]
- In 2022, there was not even one region in England where the average rent was affordable to a single woman on median earnings.[6]
- More than 1,300 homeless people are estimated to have died in the UK in 2022 (no official data are kept), equating to an average of one death every six-and-a-half hours.[7]
- In the spring of 2022, the number of people sleeping rough had risen by 34 per cent compared to the same period in the previous year.[8]
- On average, the poorest 20 per cent of private renters surrender more than half of their income to their landlords.[9]
- Renters are paying more for less: average floor space per person has shrunk from 43 square metres to 36 square metres over the past twenty years.[10]
- Almost 20 per cent of privately rented homes are thought to be in a hazardous condition.[11]
- The proportion of homeowners is gradually shrinking, while the proportion of private renters is gradually growing.[12]
- Social housing providers face a chronic lack of resources to carry out repairs, leading to an endemic of damp and mould and other forms of disrepair.

When writing about housing, the temptation to focus on London is almost overwhelming. Just as I have sometimes used 'house prices' as a byword for 'the housing crisis', I have no doubt fallen into the trap of using London as a metonym for the situation more broadly. There is some justification for the widespread obsession with the capital. Britain is a particularly unbalanced country, London often feeling more like a black hole than the centre of a stable orbit. London drives the housing crisis as a function of its centrality in the national economy. Like William Blake's mythical realm of Golgonooza, the housing crisis is an ideology and an economic phenomenon that was forged 'Here on the banks of the Thames', at the 'thund'ring Bellows on the Valley of Middlesex', but which has spread out to colonise the whole country.

This book primarily concerns Britain rather than the UK, although some data are only available on a UK-wide basis. This focus partly reflects my political objection to treating the Six Counties of Northern Ireland as being simply another part of the UK, and partly because housing in that region demands its own analysis: the law and economics of property are conditioned by colonialism, religious and political strife, and the North's relationship with the political economy of land in the Irish republic. Its economic situation contrasts sharply with that of the rest of the UK: while prices in Britain have soared to ever-new heights in recent years, homes in the Six Counties have never regained their pre-2008 values. It is a place that needs to be understood in its own terms, and it its own context.

Build More Housing?

This book seeks to short-circuit the perpetual discussion of the need to build more housing. That is because my overall argument hangs on the idea that the problem is not one of supply, but one of the cost of the housing that currently exists. There has not been a drastic change in the supply of housing per household since before the current housing crisis began. It is not the physical built environment that has changed: the houses are all still there, and population growth has not rendered them inadequate. In fact, the opposite appears to be true. A 2022 report found that the ratio of homes to the number of households has in fact grown over the lifetime of the housing crisis. Figure 1, reproduced from that report, illustrates perhaps the most important thing to understand about the housing crisis: the massive increase in housing costs over the last twenty years has coincided with a *growth* in the supply of surplus housing. Even the *Conservative Home* blog concedes that 'London now has a terrible housing crisis, even though its

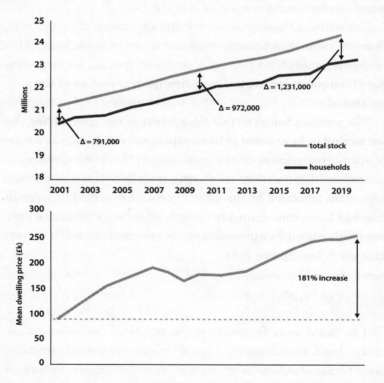

Government data shows that the UK has a surplus of dwellings relative to the number of households, and that surplus is actually increasing as housebuilding exceeds population growth (top panel). London has a higher proportion of surplus dwellings than the rest of the country. Despite this, prices continue to rise (bottom panel).[14]

population is roughly the same as it was seventy years ago' and, of course, a staggering amount of additional housing has been built in the capital since the mid 1950s.[13] Bearing this in mind, it is difficult to cast the housing crisis as a question of a sudden and severe decline in supply.

This 'under-supply' rhetoric is also weakened by the census data showing underoccupation levels. In 2021 about 70 per cent of housing in England and Wales was underoccupied, whereas less than 5 per cent was overcrowded. And yet we are constantly told that Britain does not build enough homes. This is not to say that grandparents should be turfed out of family homes to make room for overcrowded households, only that when such a large proportion – the absolute majority – of homes are now underoccupied, it is almost impossible to make an argument about scarcity and the need for a construction glut. In reality, there are plenty of homes to go around.

The problem before us therefore relates to *how* the buildings we see around us have come to be so expensive, rather than *how many* of them exist relative to the population. This book attempts to understand that question. It will therefore differ from the standard arguments advanced by mainstream economists. Despite a persistent and boisterous chorus of 'supply guys' – commentators and ostensible affordability campaigners, many of whom are aligned with the homebuilding industry and are primarily interested in the deregulation of planning law – the government's own analysis has shown that its housebuilding targets would have had a relatively small effect on housing costs, even if they had been achieved.

The 'build more housing' argument has always seemed obviously flimsy. Its strange logic is that speculative developers would build homes *in order to* devalue them: that they would somehow act against their own interests by producing enough surplus housing to bring down the average price. That would be surprisingly philanthropic behaviour. Even now (with a tolerably generous planning system that approves nearly 90 per cent of developments in England), we see phenomena such as the hoarding of developable land in order to maximise profit, and redevelopment projects that tend to turn more affordable areas into less affordable areas (rather than bringing down price through supply), because that is how the greatest profits can be realised.

Even those housing supply advocates who are not obviously shills for the building industry are unconvincing: How do they account for the staggering price rises of recent decades, despite the increasing number of homes per household (even in high-demand locations) over the same period? Indeed, how do they account for the average price rise in London during the pandemic, despite a decline in demand for housing, as – by some estimates – nearly 10 per cent of the population left the city?

Even if these advocates are right, their argument is a deeply unattractive one: in order to build enough housing to have a meaningful impact on price, we would need to build an enormous surplus of homes – in fact, many more than people need: empty homes, second homes, third homes. But, as Barnabas Calder points out in *Architecture from Pre-History to Climate Catastrophe*, constructing homes is one of the most carbon-intensive of all human activities, and buildings account for nearly 40 per cent of human greenhouse-gas emissions. Building far more homes than people need just to try to bring housing costs down – especially when we know (because of the situation that prevailed until the 1980s) that we can instead control those costs through law, regulation and policy reform – would be simply delinquent, boosting climate change for no good purpose.

This book uses the tools of Marx's critique of political economy to try to explain the housing crisis. Marx did not set out a freestanding theory of housing. At one point while writing *Capital*, presumably during a particularly idle moment in the library, he seems to have picked up a property law textbook and tried to understand the legal morass surrounding landlords' and tenants' obligations in relation to repairs, which gives me the uncanny experience of imagining Marx peering into my area of expertise when I have spent so much time rummaging around in his. But his planned later volumes of *Capital*, which might have dealt with housing markets, were not completed before his death (although Engels tackled the subject in his short polemical pamphlet *The Housing Question*). By blending the dead labour of *Capital* with the living labour of my own research, this book is an attempt to disentangle the various threads of the crisis in housing that has played such a dominant role in modern Britain.

1

The Ratchet System

'Rents are high about here. I don't know how it is exactly, but the law seems to put things up in price.'

Mr Snagsby in Charles Dickens's *Bleak House*

In April 2020, a few weeks into the Covid-19 pandemic, Ana, a member of the direct-action casework group Housing Action Southwark and Lambeth (HASL) was living in a flat with her husband and children in south London. Ana's landlord belonged to a particular group of private landlords who source their tenants from local councils' homeless populations, letting out housing that is generally of poor quality, and often setting the rent by reference to Universal Credit levels. Like almost everyone who rents privately in England and Wales, Ana held an insecure 'assured shorthold tenancy' (AST), which had, by law, been the default arrangement for private tenants since 1996. Ana and her partner worked, but their shifts were sporadic and unreliable and their wages were low, so they were also entitled to Universal Credit. Most of this went straight to their landlord.

Universal Credit is divided into a 'housing element' and a 'personal element' – but the housing element did not cover the family's full rent, so they generally had to dip into their other benefits (which were meant to cover their other living costs) and their wages to meet the shortfall. This has become increasingly common since benefit rule changes were made in 2012: tenants are faced by a pincer of ever-increasing rents, on the one hand, and cuts to Housing Benefit implemented under the austerity programme, on the other.

With this difficulty in mind, while Ana faced the fear and uncertainties of April 2020, policymakers were hurriedly trying to work out how to protect tenants from an anticipated tidal wave of evictions for pandemic-related rent arrears. The government announced an increase in the housing element of Universal Credit as a stop-gap measure. The idea was that a temporary rise in housing benefits could shield people from having to dip further into their other income, which, the government reasoned, ought to soften the impact of wage declines during lockdowns.

Unsurprisingly, Ana's landlord soon found out that the Housing Benefit rates had gone up. Ana was on a 'rolling' tenancy (her initial twelve-month tenancy had expired but continued on a month-to-month basis), and the landlord contacted the family with a proposal. He suggested that he should grant them a new year-long tenancy at a higher rent, the increase being exactly the same as the additional amount of Housing Benefit that the government had just announced. The landlord wanted this new free money that the state was offering, and he wanted it right away.

The family had two options. They were under no legal obligation to sign a new tenancy, and if they insisted on sticking with the old terms, the extra Housing Benefit would allow them to keep a little more of their wages for themselves. The benefit rise would make them a little better off financially – and this was broadly what the government was hoping to achieve. But at the same time, it was clear to them what would probably happen if they remained on the old tenancy and kept the extra money: their tenancy had expired, so the landlord was entitled to evict them on a section 21 'no fault' basis, and find a more pliable household.

On the other hand, if they agreed to the landlord's rent increase, they would not be any worse off financially than they had been before, because the government was meeting the difference, and they would at least gain the security of a new twelve-month tenancy. As HASL members explained, 'Ana has been very stressed spending the last year on a periodic tenancy (a few people in the group get stressed about being on rolling tenancies as they want stability for their children), and to be honest she didn't seem that bothered by the rent increase.' After all, the state was paying. And for people who have experienced homelessness, this sort of security – however pathetic it might seem in comparison to other forms of tenure – is important. The family signed the new tenancy agreement.

This is how the housing crisis works. Ana's case demonstrates the sublime power of the AST regime. It creates such an imbalance in bargaining positions that landlords are able to exploit even the most good-natured and tenant-friendly government policy. A measure that was supposed to reduce poverty and prevent evictions ended up simply converting welfare spending into even greater profits for a buy-to-let landlord.

At the same time, Ana's case exposes just how direct the state's role is in driving the housing crisis. The rise in Universal Credit increased the value of Ana's home because, with a rise in the amount the average benefit-recipient household could pay in housing costs, the flat could now attract a higher market rent. It both immediately paid the landlord a better monthly income and raised the value of that particular home as an asset, because it could now generate more rent in future for anyone who wanted to buy it.

The aim of this chapter is to answer Mr Snagsby's question from Dickens's 1853 novel *Bleak House*. How, exactly, does the law put rents up in price? This issue is probably the most important – and most overlooked – aspect of the housing crisis, because the private rented sector is the real villain of the piece. Not just because private renting in Britain is bad in itself, but because high rents are the engine room of the housing crisis more broadly. House prices are driven by rental yields. As I will explain in more detail below, that is the case whether you are a buy-to-let landlord, interested in the *actual* rentable value, or an owner-occupier buying the right to receive *potential* rents, or to avoid having to pay rent altogether. Rents are central to the dynamics of property pricing.

Most explanations of the housing crisis have argued that the swelling value of housing in the last few decades has been caused by extraordinary demand for housing as a commodity, and by the vast influx of capital investment after the global financial crisis. What is missing from that analysis is an exploration of *why* housing is such a profitable commodity in the first place. The private rental market is crucial in understanding the 'commodification' or 'financialisation' process. What is it that makes housing in Britain such a reliable and attractive investment? The answer is ratcheting rents. The state does not just *allow* rental yields to rise – indeed, almost *guarantee* that they will; it ensures that they rise at such a pace that residential property has become more attractive than many other forms of investment.

The Law and the Land

In October 1954 Gabriel Harrison, a young property dealer, was stuck with a piece of unprofitable land on Grafton Street in London's Mayfair (a difficulty which is unthinkable for us today). His problem was that redevelopment laws had become relatively strict during and after the Second World War, and Harrison needed a licence from the Ministry of Works in order to build on his bomb-damaged site. The ministry would not grant one, so Harrison sold the site to another developer (Harry Hyams) for £59,000. But the following week the minister for works himself, Nigel Birch MP, stood up in the House of Commons and announced that the legal requirement for building licences would be abolished just a few days later, to 'cheers from the Conservative benches'.

Harrison contacted Hyams after the minster's announcement, and Hyams offered to sell the site back to him – but for £100,000.[1]

The hapless Harrison received a lesson in the purity of the relationship between law, economics and land prices: a new law had almost doubled the value of his site. And Hyams received a lesson, too. Without the licence requirement, he was able to develop at Grafton Street himself for a profit of half a million pounds (worth many millions today), and for years afterwards received a handsome income by leasing his new building as commercial offices (he also went on, most famously, to develop London's Centre Point tower – a notorious mid-century boondoggle of prestigious-but-unwanted office space). In 2019 Westminster City Council granted planning permission for the Louis Vuitton Moët Hennessy conglomerate to build a luxury hotel on that same site on Grafton Street: a £500 million project designed by 'starchitects' Foster + Partners.[2] It is amazing what can happen to the value of the same plot of land over sixty-five years, depending on the legal and economic circumstances of the day.

The example of Grafton Street, while not directly about housing, probably sounds tediously familiar. It echoes a genre of property stories for which we seem to have a masochistic love. It is about people who bought a large house in the 1970s for a few thousand pounds (we're usually told that it 'felt very expensive at the time'), which they now own outright, and the house is worth enough to finance a small government department. These modern-day fairy tales, in which house prices play the mysterious and munificent role of the fairy godmother, appeal to our sense of awe and our sense of unfairness in equal measure. But instead of deriving some sort of moral principle, when we hear these stories we learn a simple, prosaic truth: the way in which the state regulates land and housing affects its commercial value.

The nature of this relationship between law and price is particularly clear from examples like the deregulation of the commercial property sector in the 1950s, and it is worth exploring this and similar examples before moving on to the more nuanced issue of residential land. In the post-war period the Labour government had imposed heavy restrictions on the construction of office space, broadly because a booming post-Blitz office-redevelopment industry would have been at odds with the government's social aims – particularly its intention to create a more active role for the state in planning.

In addition to the imposition of building licences discussed above, in 1948 the government imposed a 'development charge' on any increase in land value that had resulted from a grant of planning permission. This was effectively a sort-of capital gains tax in the office-development sector: the government taxed the profits generated by planning decisions. Remarkably, the charge was set at *100 per cent*.[3] For commercial developers, the government had all but taxed away the profit motive. They had made it pointless, if not impossible, for developers to profit from raising the value of land by redeveloping it as offices. This kept a firm lid on speculation in the first few years after the Second World War.

From the 1950s, however, the post-war restrictions were phased out, and a long and steady commercial property boom followed in the wake of deregulation. The 100 per cent development charge was abolished in 1951, and the Ministry of Works' requirement of building licences followed in 1954. Writing in the late 1960s, financial journalist Oliver Marriott identified a proliferation of little tycoons in commercial real estate: 'Since the war Britain is the only country in the world to have had a property boom channelling wealth into the hands of individuals on such a large scale.'[4]

But this land boom also generated significant institutional wealth, as large-scale speculative developments, freed from the post-war restrictions, began to shape many of our towns and cities. Historic England cites London's NatWest Tower and Centre Point as emblems of this post-deregulation commercial building rush, which lasted until the high interest rates and energy crisis of the early 1970s.[5] Similar examples – such as Manchester's City Tower and CIS Tower, and the suburban monolith of Tolworth Tower in Surrey – reshaped towns and cities across the country, as the legal restraints on profiting from land faded from memory.

Another example of this interplay between law and value is the controls on the height of buildings. Skyscraper construction is highly infectious. Architectural historian Manfredo Tafuri has argued that tall buildings are 'real live "bombs" with chain effects, destined to explode the entire real estate market', and we can literally watch this happening in places like London, Manchester and the United Arab Emirates. Once permission to build one tall building has been granted, other developers follow suit, and an enormous amount of profitable use from the land is suddenly unlocked as ever more layers of sellable space are created.[6]

But tall buildings tend to have negative effects on their neighbours, and the state routinely steps in to limit the height, footprint and shape of buildings to ensure that neighbouring land has access to air, sunlight and other sanitary necessities. In cities throughout the world, the state imposes such laws, which, on the one hand, restrain the potential value of skyscrapers, while, on the other, protecting the current value of surrounding land.

These development restrictions are a particularly stark illustration of the law affecting land value, because their price can be seen in real life. In the United States, for example, landowners can buy and sell the rights that come with these restrictions. In a process that architectural critic Michael Sorkin has described as reflecting 'the fungibility of air', landowners sell the rights that were designed to protect a building from the adverse effects of developments nearby; and, when this happens, we are shown exactly what those legal rights are worth in dollar terms. Remarkably, the New York City Housing Authority has decided to sell the air rights of some of its social-housing developments in order to fund essential repairs and maintenance for its low-income tenants' homes.[7]

In relation to housing, as opposed to commercial real estate, the most obvious means by which the law limits land value is through rent controls. In many cases the state sets upper limits on rents, which has a very obvious effect on land values. In Berlin, for example, tenancies are relatively secure. The law requires landlords to justify any rent increase that would take effect during the tenancy, and even those justified increases are capped at a maximum of 15 per cent over three years. In addition, a provision known as *Mietpreisbremse*, or 'rental price break', prohibits landlords from re-letting homes to new tenants above a rate set by the local authority. German landlords cannot just put the rent up, or evict and re-let, in the way that landlords in England and Wales can.

Perhaps the most notorious practitioner of gentrification-led housing-crisis exploitation is the US-based private equity firm Blackstone, whose 'buy it, fix it, sell it' model wreaked havoc in the US single-family home market in the wake of the 2008 crash, before the company's gaze turned to Europe. By 2019, nearly 70 per cent of Blackstone's residential portfolio was in Germany, the vast majority – 63 per cent of the total – in Berlin. But in 2019 Berlin's local government proposed tightening the city's rent controls. In response to these proposals – which in fact never came into full effect – Blackstone stopped buying up property in Berlin in 2018–19. As the company's annual report put it, in anodyne but telling terms, Berlin's anti-gentrification measures might 'adversely affect our results of operations'.[8]

In the British housing market, just as with the commercial building laws described earlier, the state made very powerful interventions during and after the Second World War. Full rent control had been reintroduced in 1939 to address profiteering that might result from bomb damage and a wartime halt on building. Although it was only meant to last until six months after the end of the war, it endured until Macmillan's Conservative government partially deregulated rents in 1957–58. This meant that, for a long period after the war, many rents were frozen by law at their 1939 levels, although there was some tinkering in the intervening years.

This had an obvious and serious effect on rental yields. Throughout the 1950s rents fell so low, compared to the inflation of other prices, that landlords complained they could not afford to carry out even basic repairs, and many lived in squalor as a result. When the Conservative government then temporarily removed controls from residential rents in the late 1950s, house prices in some areas jumped by up to 30 per cent. This generated a new political concern, ventilated in anxious parliamentary debates in 1964 about the soaring price of urban land and housing.[9]

The transcripts of those debates echo – in a dreary tone, full of parliamentary niceties and references to the quality of the speeches themselves – the housing discourse that we hear repeated endlessly today, most of which is frustratingly facile. An increase in homeownership is the declared ambition; but prices rise faster than people can save. Prices in urban centres are impossibly high; but green belts must be protected from development. Most landlords are good, and only a few demand exorbitant rents and inflict hardship on their tenants. Attempts to help tenants will drive landlords away and restrict availability. Social housing waiting lists will take decades to clear. Property professionals are printing unsavoury marketing material about the excellent speculative prospects of working-class areas. More homes simply must be built.

The only real flashpoint in 1964 was rent control. Some years earlier, Labour had adopted a conference motion declaring that 'private landlordism had failed',[10] and they were pushing to reverse the Tories' weakening of the wartime measures. For Labour it was an ethical question, the shadow minister – Michael Stewart, a Fabian – decrying property speculation as 'the kind of morality which rent decontrol and the general tenor of Conservative policy in so many directions over the last twelve years has produced'. The Tories' firm stance was that controls reduced supply.

But neither party was right. Rent controls, at their heart, relate to the profits that land is allowed to generate, rather than to housing supply or the personal ethics of landlords. At their most extreme – when, for example, rents cannot even cover the costs of maintenance – property becomes a liability rather than an asset, as extraordinary as that idea feels to us today. In more modest cases, rent controls reduce or limit the rental profit that housing can generate. As well as being a social policy, they represent a legal interference in the profitability of landownership. As the example of Blackstone shows us, the effects on profits are obvious and well known to investors. In Britain, of course, rent controls are entirely lacking, and there are riches to be made as a result.

Laws affecting social housing policies also have an impact on land prices. A huge amount of council housing was lost when it was sold off under the national 'right to buy' programme of the 1980s. The failure to replace it has meant that the number of council homes has remained consistently low. More than 2 million council homes have been privatised in England alone. The public's loss is the private sector's gain, as about 40 per cent of those homes are now being rented out by landlords.

This transfer of social assets into private hands has two effects. First, and most obviously, it changes the economic nature of an existing home, increasing its value dramatically. An ex-council property is no longer a home with a legally capped rent, and the money no longer goes to a ring-fenced account in the local authority's budget. Instead, a private landlord can charge whatever a tenant will pay. The home is now a profitable one, and its value is massively increased once it is placed in private hands. Given that almost a million tenanted ex-council homes in England are now valued by reference to their actual rent, and more than a million more owner-occupied homes are valued by reference to their potential rental income, the mass sell-off of council housing has unleashed an enormous amount of wealth. Millions of pounds have been added to the staggering tally of housing-based wealth discussed above through the sell-off of council housing alone.

Second, the net loss of council housing has meant that more and more people are trapped in the private rented sector. The so-called 'generation rent' – those who can neither buy nor access social housing – are forced to take tenancies. This growing captive market makes it easier for landlords to charge high or monopoly-level rents. When tenants had more options, it was far more difficult for landlords to realise those higher rents. Throughout the 1950s, for example, privately rented housing tended to be cheaper than council rents, and much of it catered to the very bottom of the market. When council housing was more readily available, many landlords were unable to compete with the new, purpose-built council homes – many of which had good-quality design and modern amenities – and instead had to cater for tenants who could not afford a council home, or were unlikely to be allocated one. But today's tenants have nowhere else to turn, and this is reflected in the extravagant prices we see in the private sector.

Perhaps the most totemic example of the effects of the selling off of social housing is in the London Borough of Southwark, which (at the time of writing) is coming to the end of massive redevelopments of two former council housing strongholds (the Heygate Estate and the Aylesbury Estate, both near Elephant and Castle). As the council buildings fell to make way for new private developments, we saw those two effects in action: in Elephant Park (on the site of Heygate) the former council land is now so valuable that the very cheapest options – small, single-occupancy flats sold under the 'shared ownership' scheme – cost more than half a million pounds. Meanwhile, the displacement of former residents, particularly those who must now rent privately, intensifies the need for housing in the areas to which they have had to move.

Of course, none of this was an accident. At the start of the process, a Southwark Council official explained: 'We need to have a wider range of people living in the borough . . . social housing generates people on low incomes coming in and that generates poor school performances, middle class people stay away.'[11]

Slightly subtler examples of the interplay between housing law and land prices include the 'Help to Buy' policy, introduced when housebuilders suffered shock losses after the 2008 global financial crisis. The government brought in sensationally generous mortgage loans for first-time buyers, but only for new-build housing. Seemingly oblivious to the climate emergency, this policy ensured that the greatest profits could be realised by building new homes aimed at first-time buyers. This boosted the value of developable land. A House of Lords report in 2022 found that this apparently benign policy, designed to help younger households meet spiralling costs, had in fact simply inflated the price of land.[12] Wherever we look, we can see the relationship between law and profitability at work.

The Rent Is Too Damn High

What makes the situation in Britain so unusual is that it contradicts the most common explanations of rising housing costs. A long-held view, discernible even in nineteenth-century writing about housing, is that rents rise when improvements are made, because those improvements increase the value of the commodity. This still holds true in cities where tenancies are regulated, such as Berlin, Vienna and Copenhagen, where anti-gentrification campaigners are often in the odd position of having to fight against improvements to their own homes in order to prevent landlords from obtaining a legal basis for putting the rent up. But across Britain rents are constantly rising, even as housing conditions are in decline: the government's own figures show that, in 2019, some 13 per cent of privately rented homes (more than half a million) had at least one defect so severe that it posed a serious threat to the tenant's health or safety.[13] We have also seen a decline in space and living standards; more and more people live in shared homes, and living rooms are converted into bedrooms. One of the peculiarities of Britain's housing crisis is that rents continue to rise even as housing quality plummets: 'improvements' offer no explanatory clue.

Another well-established explanation for rising housing costs is 'rent-gap theory', which holds that prices go up when landowners close the gap between the revenue generated by the previously existing use of the land – which attracted a lower rent – and the new, higher yield. An obvious example is that of knocking down some old industrial buildings or terraced streets to build luxury flats. Again, while we certainly see a great deal of gentrification in urban centres, this does not adequately explain why rents rise so consistently, even without landlords and landowners having to pursue the traditional rent-gap-closing activities of evictions, redevelopment and repurposing.

Rent-gap theory originated with geographer Neil Smith in 1979, and his work has been described as the 'sacred text for economic theories of gentrification'.[14] In short, a rent gap exists where there is a difference between the current rental yield of a particular piece of real estate and the potential rent that the same property would be capable of generating if its nature, condition or usage were changed. Where such gaps exist, the economic incentive is to close them: to achieve that higher potential rent by putting the land to its 'highest and best use'. Smith's original argument related to post-war cities in wealthy nations. He theorised that there were many places where profits could be made through buying land in distressed areas and redeveloping it. This has become a common tool for explaining rising housing costs.

But rent-gap theory does not adequately explain how the housing crisis works in the particular context of contemporary

Britain. For one thing, rents have risen almost across the board, rather than in specific locations where deprivation is forced to make way for the new and expensive. Data from the 2021 census showed that 'housing affordability worsened in 300 out of 331 (91%) local authorities', while average house prices 'increased in 96% of local authority districts in England and Wales'.[15] It cannot possibly be the case that virtually the whole country is perpetually and simultaneously levelling up, putting all of its land to a higher or better use. Second, and more fundamentally, rent-gap theory does not work in a context in which there is no barrier to raising rents.

The working assumption in rent-gap theory is that a gap emerges because there has been some obstacle preventing the landowner from closing it, which is then overcome. As Brett Christophers explains, 'If it *were* straightforward to close rent gaps, they would not widen and then persist in the relatively durable forms in which Smith and other urban scholars have depicted them; rather, they would be closed without ado.'[16] But in Britain it *is* straightforward to close rent gaps.

Of course, it is difficult to throw up a large new housing development, but in a jurisdiction with no rent controls and virtually no security of tenure, landlords can put prices up so quickly and so consistently that we do not tend to see the chasm between actual and potential rents that forms the basis of rent-gap theory. The AST regime means that rents on existing buildings can rise unencumbered, quickly matching or exceeding the rents prevailing in the surrounding area.

In other words, attempts to use rent-gap theory to explain what is currently happening in Britain are misguided. Economist Phillipe Askenazy offers gentrification in London as an emblematic example of an area (Marylebone) becoming fashionable, and thus more expensive.[17] Either through the amelioration of local facilities and infrastructure, improvements to Marylebone's housing stock itself, or a combination of the two, a rent gap, Askenazy argues, is closed and a higher price realised.

But there are many parts of Britain – particularly in south-east England and major urban centres – where rents have rocketed, but where those amelioration factors have not only been absent, but have reversed. Since the austerity regime began, local services have been cut, investment has been inadequate, and transport and infrastructure have been in a state of managed decline – in many ways, our cities are becoming worse places to live; but rents have continued to increase. They rise on existing residential buildings without any significant improvement to the homes – and they do so extraordinarily steeply.

Our housing crisis does not fit into this neat economic model. Instead, what is happening is mainly a consequence of a deliberate government policy of state-backed rent-raising.

How does this happen? Through a system of housing law, the government has replicated a system of previously illegal activities that took place in the 1950s and 1960s, in which thuggish landlords would bypass rent controls and 'sweat' their tenants to extract the highest possible rents. The state has now adopted the practices of the twentieth century's most notorious landlords, turning them into the fundamental basis of the current landlord–tenant relationship.

During most of the twentieth century, it was relatively difficult for landlords to raise the rent of a sitting tenant. Landlords started to look for ways of circumventing this obstacle because, if they were able to get rid of a secure tenant with a controlled rent, there was a great deal of money to be made. This was because, in 1957, the Conservative government had weakened the private-sector rent controls that had been applied during the war, and this deregulation took place at a moment of high demand for housing and a growing number of households (particularly in London). These circumstances created particularly high demand for accommodation in cities at the same time that rent controls were being loosened, leading to a strong upward pressure on prices. This meant that, by granting a new tenancy after 1957 – or 'persuading' a tenant to give up an existing one – and having shrugged off the pre-1957 controls that had frozen rents at their pre-war levels, landlords could now achieve average rent increases of 145 per cent.[18]

Of course, the relatively secure tenancies that were mandatory at the time meant that landlords could not simply kick out a pre-1957 tenant and re-let the property. Unlike in the case of Ana, discussed above, if a 1950s tenant was unwilling to sign away their existing tenancy, the landlord was stuck with a sitting tenant with a very low controlled rent, set at a level that had been fixed before the Blitz.

Some landlords – most notoriously west London's Peter Rachman – resorted to violence and intimidation. Through acts of physical hostility, such landlords increase their profits by forcing sitting tenants either to sign up to new, de-controlled tenancy agreements, or to leave and make way for someone else. Rachman's methods included sending thugs to intimidate tenants, sprinkling itching powder on beds and toilet seats, leaving dead rats in properties, removing doors – and in one case even removing the roof. The legal circumstances also required him to create complex webs of companies that made it so difficult to police breaches of housing conditions – for example, stinking drains – that tenants in rent-controlled accommodation would leave in disgust before any action could be taken.

But today's tenants lack the security and rent controls of the 1950s and 1960s, and there is no longer any need to resort to violence to raise the rent. The modern landlord's absolute legal *right* to make someone homeless – rather than the threat that they might do so *unlawfully* – is sufficient to persuade today's tenants to agree to the landlord's price, as Ana's family decided to do. The sheer power that the post-1980s housing law regime granted to landlords was designed with this economic factor in mind: the main purpose of the Thatcherite recasting of housing rights was to establish the conditions for the creation, and then the constant expansion, of a profitable housing market. The way this was achieved was by regularising the previously unlawful system of cowing tenants into paying more.

The 1988 Housing Act created the 'assured shorthold tenancy', which could be brought to an end upon the expiry of the contractual term (with an initial six-month term being the legal minimum), or at any point thereafter, on a 'no-fault' basis and under an accelerated repossession procedure (this is what is known as a 'section 21' eviction: the ending of an assured shorthold tenancy on the ground that the contract has expired). In short, it introduced highly unstable short-term tenancies in the private sector. The 1996 Housing Act then made these tenancies the default.

These very short, insecure tenancies are a problem because there is, in general, a constant upward pressure on rents. The private rented sector is not a market in which competition tends to bring down price; landlords are not subject to competitive forces. Instead, the absolute necessity of housing to meet basic human needs, and the fact that many people need to live near their places of work, means that urban rents tend towards the maximum level that tenants are able to pay.

It is often impossible for tenants to shop around for appropriate shelter, as it is impossible to produce more local land with homes on it in order to undercut other landlords. When the landlord announces a rent increase, the tenant cannot simply say, 'I'll find somewhere cheaper.' Instead, landlords are able to withhold access to housing until the tenant either agrees to the landlord's price or is forced to give up and live somewhere else entirely. The upper limit on rent is therefore determined not by competition, but by the maximum amount tenants are willing to pay to live in a particular location.

This was a point on which Adam Smith and Karl Marx agreed. In *The Wealth of Nations*, Smith argued that rent was 'naturally a

monopoly price'. Marx developed this insight, arguing that housing rents in particular are 'only explicable by monopoly conditions'.
The intense need for housing, coupled with landowners' ability to
withhold access, means that price does not find its upper limit
through competition between landlords, but rather through the
amount that tenants (at a particular location, and under given social
circumstances) are able to pay for shelter. This is particularly true,
Marx claimed, in cities: 'landed property . . . by its very situation in
populated areas carries a monopoly'.[19]

That is why, all over the world, governments generally step in
to impose some sort of legal brake on this process – whether in the
form of security of tenure, a rent regulation measure, or both – to
prevent the frenzied price rises that can occur when housing markets are left unchecked. As we have seen, it was by bypassing these
measures, through force and intimidation, that landlords in the
1950s and '60s were able to raise the rent whenever they wanted to;
but there are no longer any such protections to bypass. For today's
landlords, like Ana's, this rent-raising power is baked into the
system. Whenever there is the possibility of realising an increased
rent – through increased wages, local price rises, the general constant upward pressure that comes with monopoly prices, social
acceptance of higher rent levels, or simply a suspicion that a tenant
is able to pay more – a landlord is very well-placed to demand it.

If the tenant refuses, eviction can follow within months. While
these demands tend to be made when tenancies come up for
renewal, they can in theory be made at almost any time, as Ana's
case shows. We have a system of legally sanctioned sweating, as
opposed to illegal sweating: the whole system of private tenancy
rights functions to allow landlords to extract the maximum possible
rent from sitting tenants, and not just from re-lets. This is how the
law facilitates rent increases.

There was a curious phenomenon during the Rachman scandal
when hundreds of tenants from all over the country wrote to the

parliamentary committee charged with investigating rack-renting, convinced that Rachman himself was their landlord. His crimes were so familiar that it hardly seemed to matter to these tenants that Rachman had only operated in a small corner of west London, and was in fact already dead. Today, the opposite seems to be true. All assured shorthold tenants genuinely are the subjects of Rachman-style sweating. Today's tenants are all but powerless to say no to a rent increase, because they all know what might happen if they do.

But this relationship is now completely normalised, to the extent that its scandalous nature has become invisible to us. The type of power imbalance that caused nationwide outrage in the 1960s is taken today as a fact of life. This is the key point about the role of section 21 within assured shorthold tenancies. It is not so much that so-called 'no-fault evictions' are unfair and distressing, or that insecure housing has all sorts of dreadful personal and social con-sequences – though all of these things are, of course, the case. Instead, assured shorthold tenancies are what allow rents to rise so exceptionally rapidly. The prevalence of short-term tenancies means that there is no brake on the general tendency of rents to rise when left unchecked.

This economic aspect of section 21 is not very well understood. In 2019, just after the Labour Party's pre-election announcement that it would abolish 'no-fault' evictions, I was at a meeting where I told John Healey (then the shadow housing minister) that he had in effect committed the party to reintroducing a form of rent regu-lation by the back door (because, without the possibility of section 21 evictions, rents can only be raised if the tenancy agreement allows for it, or under a little-used statutory procedure). He looked at me as if I had grown an extra head. Both Labour and the Conservative government – which matched Labour's section 21 pledge in its own manifesto – seemed to think that the abolition of 'no-fault' evictions was a fluffy, family-friendly policy, rather than a radical dismantling of the longstanding Thatcherite framework of housing law, and a key part of its strategy for keeping rents high.

It is a striking fact that possession claims – the means by which tenants are evicted through the court process – have steadily declined throughout the housing crisis. But this does not disprove the point about legalised rack-renting. It is not a process that requires millions of tenants to be thrown out onto the street. In chess, the king is never taken. But the absolute right to evict – the state's guarantee that landlords can take possession very quickly – puts landlords in an overwhelmingly powerful bargaining position. Housing insecurity produces a silent compulsion enforcing rental discipline. As many of us know from experience, most landlords will simply give tenants a new agreement to sign, or simply announce that the rent is going up. These take-it-or-leave-it offers are backed up by a tacit understanding that eviction might easily follow right away if a new rent is not agreed, and then paid like clockwork. Tenants who wish to stay in their homes are left with no choice but to accept these increases, or to find somewhere else to live, without the landlord needing to take any active steps towards evicting them. With this extraordinary legal tool at their disposal, landlords have made regular and sharp rent increases seem like a self-evident law of nature.

Housing Benefit: The Landlord Subsidy

But it is not enough that rents can notionally be increased under a particular legal system. It is all very well that the state promises landlords they have an absolute right to kick out any tenant who does not agree to a rent increase, but if the tenant (or their replacement) cannot pay the higher rent, there is little benefit to the landlord. It only matters – rents only go up in reality – if landlords' demands for new, higher rents are met. If the ratchet system is going to work, the government needs to find a way to ensure that Britain's tenants meet landlords' ever-increasing financial demands.

It was part of the redesign of the housing framework during the Thatcher governments that the state shifted its activity from the direct provision of council housing to that of supporting the growing number of private tenants through Housing Benefit. Under a benefits system first introduced in 1981 – though much expanded and changed over the next forty years – the state undertook to pay a portion of the nation's rent. For financially eligible tenants, Housing Benefit – now known as Local Housing Allowance or Universal Credit (Housing Element) – pays all or some of the rent; until 2012, the amount available was tied to the local market rent.

The fact that Housing Benefit was tied to the market rate of local rents, coupled with the way in which the AST regime allowed rents to rise rather than restraining them, created excellent conditions for a vicious circle. Rents crept upwards, Housing Benefit levels were forced to rise in response, and landlords then dug a little deeper as they discovered that tenants were able to meet the demand made of them.

This should have been obvious from the start: in 1991 the Conservative housing minister, George Young, explained that Housing Benefit might 'take the strain' where rents became unaffordable – an extraordinary thing to say at a time when the government was in the process of dismantling the rent-stabilisation mechanisms of the private sector. It could have come as no surprise that the Housing Benefit bill – the transfer of wealth from the state to private landlords – exploded from the 1990s onwards. As rents rose, the state guaranteed that a proportion of the working class would always be able to meet those rising costs by underwriting a large part of the national rent bill.

Indeed, there was historical precedent for this. Under the Poor Laws, through which local parishes paid the rents of many of the poorest households, a major cause of the massive rent inflation of the early nineteenth century was that 'landlords could be reasonably confident that if they fixed rents too high for the labourer to afford, the parish would indemnify [*sic*]'.[20] As the *Morning Chronicle* put it in 1850, 'There is no kind of property which gives a higher rent or of which the rent is better paid than that of houses occupied by the lower orders. When the landlord once adopts rigorous measures to enforce his demands, the parish takes good care that the payment shall afterwards be regularly made.'[21]

The economic effect here is clear: if the cost of rented housing is, in many urban areas, a monopoly price determined – where rent regulation measures are absent – only by society's ability to pay, rents will rise continuously if and when the government guarantees to underwrite them. The state itself has enabled, even sponsored, the dramatic rise in rents that lies at the heart of the housing crisis.

As Anna Minton has argued, this system is exacerbated by the way in which the Housing Benefit regime interacts with the uneven spread of wealth in Britain. In high-rent areas, Housing Benefit rates are necessarily higher. This means that some councils have more clout – more spending power – than others when it comes to rehousing people under the homelessness provisions. This creates a domino effect, in which demand for housing is pushed outwards: if a council (say, Kensington and Chelsea) has a high rate of local housing allowance, it can afford to place a family in a cheaper area (Watford, for example) more easily than Watford Council itself could afford to place one of its own households. Watford is then required to look to somewhere cheaper for its own households – and so on.[22] Again, Housing Benefit rules – while they may have been designed to alleviate severe poverty – merely serve to ensure that housing costs can keep rising around the country when they interact with the system of untrammelled rents in the private sector.

In 2012 there was a dramatic shift. The government both reduced the rate of Housing Benefit that it would pay in every local authority area and capped the annual increase based on the consumer price index, even if rent rises exceeded inflation. This meant that, under the austerity regime, housing costs began to eat up an ever larger share of the resources of the privately renting population, while an increasingly smaller proportion was paid by the state. For about twenty years, the state itself had directly fed a dynamic of rents being ratcheted upwards by footing a significant part of the bill; but over the next ten years it fell increasingly to tenants themselves to meet landlords' ever-increasing demands for higher rents by giving up a higher proportion of their income, sacrificing their own living standards at the altar of year-on-year rent increases. Trust for London has found that Londoners paid an average of 45.3 per cent of their *pre-tax* income on rent in 2021 (governments worldwide tend to use 30 per cent of income as a rough estimate of whether housing is 'affordable').[23] Meanwhile, the Institute for Fiscal Studies has found a very significant increase in the number of households with a shortfall between their rent and the value of their Housing Benefit.[24]

The state does not pay everyone's rent. In 2022 Housing Benefit paid £23.4 billion of the estimated £63 billion national rent bill – a little over one-third.[25] While this is a significant proportion, the benefits system alone is not directly responsible for increasing housing costs across the board. But the privately rented housing for which LHA is available, being the cheapest by definition, forms the bottom layer of the housing market in any given area. The cost of rent in this base layer – the absolute minimum that any landlord might realistically demand for their property – has gradually risen as Housing Benefit has kept pace with local market rents, and then with inflation.

It is uncontroversial to say that better-quality housing will attract a higher rent than its lower-quality comparator. Thus, anything that is better than the cheapest form of housing available in a particular area will tend to be more expensive. That being the case, as rents and Housing Benefit at the bottom of the market rise, the cost of the better-quality housing above them will rise too.

In this sense, this book parts company with most accounts of the housing crisis. Explanations based on 'financialisation' or the 'commodification' of housing tend to take a 'top down' approach: huge amounts of investment in luxury housing by the extremely rich displace the merely *very* rich, who are forced (it is argued) into slightly cheaper areas, displacing those on the next rung down, and so on, driving up demand and prices. But equally important, if not more so, is the rising tide of the bottom of the market. It is the fact that the state underwrites constant rent increases from the bottom up that has made housing in Britain such a profitable investment in the first place. Without unregulated rents on working-class housing, propped up by theoretically limitless public spending on Housing Benefit, the cost of middle-class housing would not have risen as steeply and reliably as it has.

We would not, in that case, have seen the reliable rises in house prices and frenzied speculation that have defined the housing market for the last twenty years. In other words, if it were not for the steadily rising rents and Housing Benefit at the bottom of the market, the conditions would not exist for the glittering moneybox towers along the River Thames, the palaces around Hyde Park, the expats' enclaves in Surrey, or the speculative luxury developments in towns and cities around the country.

This deliberate policy of massive state spending to ensure rent growth makes Britain particularly unusual. As Marx pointed out as far back as 1844, landlords' interests are inimical to pretty much everyone else's: tenants want rents to be lower; capital wants both wages (and thus residential rents) and commercial rents to be lower; and governments often tend to be more interested in enacting this rare bipartisan demand than in promoting the interests of landed property.[26] David Harvey (writing before the present housing crisis, in 1982) argued that – when faced with landowners competing for enhanced rents – states have generally intervened 'to counter the incoherency and . . . speculative fevers land markets are periodically heir to'.[27]

But the British state has intervened to do the exact opposite. By keeping rented housing reliably profitable, it has fuelled demand for housing investment. While many governments of powerful capitalist states, such as Germany, tend to keep housing costs at least somewhat under control (ensuring that domestic capital has a smaller wage bill), the British state since the 1980s has been ploughing money into a system of constantly rising private rents, thereby boosting property investment. Britain has deployed enormous state spending in propping up its own housing crisis.

What Is a House Price?

Many have pointed out that housing nowadays tends to be treated as a financial asset. Like stocks, shares and bonds, it is traded as a commodity that generates returns and stores wealth. This approach to housing provides us with a very useful framework: by looking at how other forms of financial asset work, we can see exactly how it is that housing has become so very expensive. What takes place is a process called 'capitalisation', a process that Marx explains in volume III of *Capital*.*

Capitalisation is a method of working out what a financial asset is worth by establishing its yield (rent, in the case of housing), and comparing it to the returns available from other forms of investment elsewhere in the economy (usually expressed as interest rates). In other words: How does housing compare with other forms of investment? Where should I put my money to get the best

---

* For those familiar with volume I of *Capital* this may be confusing, as 'capitalisation' has a completely different meaning there. Marx, with his characteristic clarity and courtesy towards his reader, uses the same term to mean two totally different things.

return? Like so many of Marx's insights, this topic is as technical and cheerless as it is important and revelatory. Capitalisation is crucial to understanding what has been happening over the last few decades, as well as what might happen next.

The conventional account of the housing crisis, certainly on the left, is that properties have come to be seen as assets first and homes second. This change in attitude has engendered a new, intense demand among buyers that has gone hand-in-hand with financial deregulation, and with an excess of money floating around world markets with nowhere else to go.[28] But this interpretation puts the cart before the horse, arguing that all of this investment ended up in housing, and that prices rose as a result.

Why housing? And why is capital suddenly more attracted to British housing than it was before? We have to examine why people want to buy the housing commodity in the first place. The short answer to that is that rental yields here rise dependably, year on year, which makes housing a money-generation machine. Perpetually rising rents, when compared with the actual and expected performance of other forms of financial investment, are what make housing so uniquely attractive.

Why place so much emphasis on rent when less than 20 per cent of households are private renters? The answer is that rent *is* house prices, and housing costs *are* the housing crisis. In other words, rental yields are critical in determining the value of land. It feels like a counterintuitive method: we are so used to thinking about house prices as logically prior to and independent of rent. But even in the nineteenth century Marx was chiding those who saw rents as being derived from house prices, rather than the other way around. Rent is a far more ancient concept than house prices (even the Domesday Book contains references to money rents), and is the logically prior one.

The development of the system of buying and selling land in the early modern period, rather than holding land as an ancestral right, initially took the form of trading pre-existing rental rights and obligations. Those money rents had developed throughout the Middle Ages, as wages became the fundamental basis of the economy, and as financial payments connected with the use of land had come to replace other, much older forms of feudal obligation. While we tend to think of those pre-monetary feudal duties in terms of labour and military service, idiosyncratic examples of ancient rents included compulsory hangman duty, holding King John's seasick head on Channel crossings, and – in the unfortunate case of a Suffolk tenant named Rolland – making a leap, a whistle and a fart on Christmas day in the presence of the king (later switched for a more mundane cash obligation).[29]

Paying a monetary tribute to a landowner for the use of land is an inherent and plainly observable phenomenon under both feudalism and capitalism. And a system of trading the rights to receive those rental payments (or buying the right to avoid having to pay rent by owning land), thereby fixing a price that reflects those rights, flows from the rental system.

While Marx never undertook any systematic study of housing markets, and most of his writing about land and rent focused on agricultural rather than residential property, what is clear from his work is that the purchase price of land is a claim upon anticipated rental yields. As he wrote in *Capital*, volume III: 'The price of land is nothing but the capitalized and thus anticipated rent'; to buy property merely 'procures a title for the purchaser to receive the annual rent'.[30] As David Harvey puts it, 'land is treated as a pure financial asset which is bought and sold according to the rent it yields . . . what is traded is a claim upon future revenues, which means a claim upon future profits from the use of the land'.[31]

From this perspective we can see why the fact that rents rise so quickly is crucial in understanding the housing crisis: house prices are based on the rising rents of an unencumbered private rented sector. Anticipated growth in rents is the index by which house prices rise so quickly and reliably – and those rising prices are the reason why there is such high demand among buyers. Rising rents translate into rising house prices.

But how does this occur, in practice? Take, for example, the case of a house that generates £1,000 per month (£12,000 per year) in rent. If you wanted to buy that house – which is, in effect, to buy a legally enforceable right to receive that rental income – you would have to work out how much such an entitlement is worth in cash terms. You could do that by working out how much money you would have to invest in other parts of the economy to achieve similar sorts of return.

If we assume, for example, that the interest rate is 5 per cent, you would know that, in order to receive £12,000 per year by lending money out at interest, you would have to lay out £240,000. The seller of the house would need to make sure that potential buyers' money would be no better off if it were lent out, kept in a savings account or invested elsewhere: the price of the house must compete with other profitable activities. The house must therefore also be worth about £240,000 as a financial asset, regardless of whether it is being sold to a landlord or an owner-occupier.

Under current conditions of rising rents, the price would reflect not just the £12,000 that the landlord would receive in year one, but £12,500 in year two, £13,000 in year three, and so on. If you bought the house today, you would be charged £240,000 plus an amount representing the likely appreciation in rent in the future. This is what is meant by 'capitalisation': deriving the price of an asset by reference to its yields and looking at those yields in the context of the rates of return on other forms of investment. This, Marx argues, applies to assets such as land just as much as it applies to revenue-generating financial instruments such as stocks and bonds.

This regime of homeowning as a financial endeavour (rather than simply of buying a place to live) is generalised. It is not only landlords who treat housing as an investment that produces actual rental yields; there being no formal distinction between homes sold to landlords and homes sold to residents – all homes are 'capitalised' by reference to their anticipated rental yields, or at least by comparison to the value of homes that are sold for rent. Almost every home could at least potentially be rented out, if that was something the homeowner wanted or needed to do; thus, almost every home has a potential rentable value, and, on a Marxist analysis, it is that yield that determines the financial value of property.

This leads to a peculiar situation in which the financial players in one of the most significant parts of Britain's economy are predominantly homeowners and petty landlords, rather than corporations and large-scale investors. While there have been attempts to pin Britain's housing crisis on shadowy international finance houses, the daily battles of the housing crisis are in fact fought between ordinary people competing over the right to receive the riches that flow from property ownership.

Capitalisation is also a useful concept regardless of the relatively small number of homes that are in reality rented out, because mortgages behave in a very similar way to rents. When a mortgage lender values a house, it is working out the yield that the borrower would pay back to the lender, based in turn on the limits of what buyers are willing and able to pay for the particular property, and whether that income represents an acceptable and secure return on its loan. We can treat mortgaged homeowners as being, in essence, another form of rent-payer, and understand the house prices of owner-occupied homes by 'capitalisation' in just the same way. This, of course, is why mortgage rates and products are so important: the available products determine the price that the average buyer is able to pay, based on household income and interest rates.

Harvey's description of land as a 'pure financial asset' as far back as 1982 might seem to be at odds with today's dominant narrative about the very recent financialisation of housing. There is a common complaint that housing has moved 'from a basic need to a financial asset'. But a Marxist understanding would be that, under capitalism, housing has *always* been a financial asset. It is a thing that everyone needs, which tends to be withheld from us unless we can meet a certain price, and in this sense it has always been 'commodified'. In the nineteenth century, Marx pointed out that housing profits are made not by producing new homes but by creating the conditions in which residential rental yields will rise.[32] Land and housing are, and always were, forms of capital – what Marxists would call 'fictitious capital', consisting of a legal title and a claim on future income that is similar to stocks or securities. Privately owned homes have always been traded as such.[33]

Many commentators complain that the current system of housing costs represents a separation between the 'use value' of housing (its value as a unit of accommodation) and its 'exchange value' (as a commercial asset).[34] But they misunderstand what Marx meant by those terms, and it is worth focusing on this point. 'Use value' in the Marxist sense does not mean the price that housing would attract if it were treated purely as a home and not as a financial asset (indeed, such a price could only ever be a highly theoretical thought experiment, given that housing has always been treated as a financial asset under capitalism). Instead, 'use value' has nothing to do with 'price', but instead has a meaning similar to 'utility': What is it used for? Commodities may have more than one use value or utility. Just as a soy bean could have two or more use values (I might make it into tofu, or I might sell it to a farmer as livestock feed), landed property is capable of accommodating someone, functioning as a store of value, and/or generating a stream of rental income for the owner. This has been the case for centuries.

The root cause of the problem is not that there is now suddenly more greed, more loose money circulating due to quantitative easing (state-printed money, much of which has found its way into real estate), or even more deregulated credit. On the contrary: the availability of credit, lent at interest, tends to indicate that finance capital is confident that there are profits to be made from some inherently worthwhile investment. Instead, the current problem is that the rent-ratcheting system described above makes housing in Britain an incredibly good investment. The total national rent bill has more than doubled since the global financial crisis: from £27.8 billion in 2008 to £63 billion in 2022.[35] When rents rise that reliably, they are translated into ever-growing prices of residential land. By this mechanism – a direct consequence of the Thatcherite system of government-backed price increases in the private rented sector – housing since the late 1980s has become an incomparably secure and fruitful form of investment.

In addition, we have seen a long period of very low interest rates. As set out above, in the approach to this problem made through the lens of capitalisation, interest rates are one of the variables that determine the value of assets, including house prices. But things start to get even more interesting when interest rates begin to move. If we use the same figures as above, where a piece of land is generating a steady annual income of £12,000 in rent, it is worth £240,000 while interest rates stand at 5 per cent. If interest rates fall to 2.5 per cent, a yield of £12,000 from investments elsewhere in the economy would require a layout of £480,000, instead of £240,000 – and the seller of the land will therefore be able to raise the price, because what they are selling is a right to receive a yearly income of the very same £12,000.

At a stroke, the land has doubled in price because the interest rate has fallen – though these processes of course tend to work themselves through the system much more slowly in the real world. On the other hand, the price will fall when – as now – interest rates are rising. It is easy to understand why so many people are worried about house prices: both of the factors that determine price – well-founded expectations of ever-rising rents, and very low interest rates – have driven rising land prices for many years. But things are beginning to change.

The speed and reliability with which rents rise; the short periods of their payment (generally monthly or weekly); the government's promise to help many people to meet those rents; the easy and effective mechanisms for overcoming interruptions in receiving rents, such as eviction and replacement with paying tenants; the favourable comparison of private renal income to other forms of profit-bearing investment – all of these factors converge to transform housing into a financial golden goose.

For the last few decades it would almost be wrong to think of it as speculation, given that the system is designed to ensure and maintain the rising value of the nation's housing. When Gordon Brown was advertising contracts to build and own schools and hospitals through New Labour's PFI initiative in 2000, he told investors: 'These are core services which the government is statutorily bound to provide, and for which demand is virtually insatiable. Your revenue stream is ultimately backed by the government. Where else are you going to get a long-term business opportunity like that?'[36]

A good response might have been 'house-price growth'.

2

A Longer View

The desire of Profitte greatly increaseth Buyldinges . . . Thes sorte of covetous Buylders exacte great renttes, and daiely do increase them, in so muche that a poore handie craftsman is not able by his paynefull laboure to pay the rentte of a small Tenement and feede his familie.

Seventeenth-century tract

In March 2021, during one of the numerous Covid lockdowns, I went to court to try to stop the eviction of a number of 'property guardians' who were hiring living spaces in a disused office building. It was an odd day in many respects. Covid restrictions meant that only a few of us were allowed in the building, so some of the occupiers could not even be inside while their case was being decided. The rest of us sat in court masked, distanced and uneasy. Many of us had not left home for days. The property guardianship company was so committed to evicting the occupiers that they had hired a very senior lawyer – a Queen's Counsel – to argue the case for them. The QC was bullish: before the hearing he had unsettled me by repeatedly accusing me, in a foul-tempered tone, of being an 'absolute disgrace' for raising various legal arguments on behalf of the guardians. And his behaviour agitated the occupiers, too. We lost, and we left court feeling winded and dismayed.

But the case was then subject to a number of complex appeal hearings about the legal nature of property guardianships. What had started out looking like a relatively simple matter about an eviction spun out into a detailed examination of the history and development of property rights in England, dating all the way back to the medieval period. In order to work out whether the property guardians could stay, it was necessary to think about the essence of landownership itself.

Reading about the housing crisis now, it would be easy to reach the conclusion that 'commodification' and 'financialisation' were invented around 2008. Some memories stretch further back, as far as the 1980s and the national 'right to buy' scheme. Looking back at the long development of land rights, however, it becomes clear that this perspective ignores the sophisticated history of property speculation that has unfolded since the seventeenth century.

Similarly, some commentators would have you believe that the reason for your high rent or unaffordable mortgage is intimately connected with international finance capital, and that there are thoroughly modern explanations for the current situation. But this misconstrues how property rights and capitalism have developed hand-in-glove over hundreds of years. Today's housing crisis is merely a continuation of much older processes.

Others make the opposite mistake of arguing that the system of landownership in Britain is still essentially feudal in nature. Sometimes this idea derives from freeman on the land–type conspiracy theorists, but sometimes it is articulated by serious writers and commentators who ought to know better, such as those arguing for tax reform, roaming rights or rewilding projects. True enough, all land is technically still owned by the Crown, and some wealthy landowners still hold noble titles. Indeed, some landholdings date back to the Norman Conquest. But the modern system of landownership in Britain is absolutely an expression of capitalist social and economic relations, and needs to be understood as such. Although the Crown may own the land, the modern state is not only subject to powerful legal restrictions, but has also developed its own deep ideological commitment to private property rights. The interrelationship between capitalism and property law has produced the housing regime that we see today.

Early capitalism was concerned with landlords' rights to extract ever more value from agrarian land, and that agricultural dimension has been the focus of much historical and theoretical debate. But the development of agrarian land rights and practices also had knock-on effects on housing. As the value of domestic agriculture went into decline, largely due to the successes of colonialism in producing wealth abroad, and as the mass of working people became increasingly large, urban and propertyless, the importance of the housing aspect of land rights increased. Increasing amounts of both land and people were encompassed by the principles of commodification. Housing, along with everything else, was exposed to all of the various crises and contradictions of capitalism itself.

Many good histories of housing policy have been written, and it would be pointless to try to condense that literature here. Instead, as well as setting the context for the current crisis, this historical chapter seeks to establish three things. First, it is important to note that the capitalist treatment of land is in fact a regime with deep historical roots, rather than an innovation of the twenty-first century. Second, the near-death of private landlordism in the twentieth century shows how tantalisingly close we came to achieving a better world. Third, the more recent policy history shows us how deep-set are the causes of the failure to produce effective ideas for tackling the housing crisis: the *longue durée* of our current problems encompasses an ideological void that has existed for many decades.

The Dawn of Commodification

In the sixteenth and seventeenth centuries, in many parts of the country, building homes was a criminal offence. That was because, until the Stuart Restoration in 1660, the rather crude assumption was that the government could curb population growth simply by refusing to allow sufficient accommodation to exist. The Tudor period had seen a population boom caused by land enclosures, urbanisation and the release of former religious communities from their vows of chastity during the dissolution of the monasteries (while he wrote copiously about the first two factors, it seems that Marx failed to consider the sexual appetites of demobilised monks and nuns). Various laws and royal proclamations prohibited the laying of any new foundations within three miles of London's city walls, as well as banning the subdivision of existing homes within that city. At the same time, across the country it was illegal to build cottages anywhere unless they had a minimum of four acres to support them.[1]

Of course, the fact that something was illegal did not mean that it did not happen, and tenements, rookeries and irregular dwellings sprung up in many population centres. While unlicensed new buildings of this kind were very common (it is possible that the building controls operated more as a sort of stealth tax than a sincere prohibition), their construction did carry a significant degree of personal risk. Records of criminal proceedings in the Court of Aldermen (an ancient City of London body) and the Court of Star Chamber show that there were occasional sprees of imprisonments and finings of property developers, accompanied by the tearing down of unlicensed homes.[2]

Both the law and society disdained the construction of new housing, badly needed though it was. The risk of demolition meant that new homes tended to be extremely cheaply built, hidden in dark, out-of-sight corners, or patchwork additions crammed onto existing dwellings. There were exceptions, of course, and the authorities were particularly untroubled by grand new houses built by wealthier landowners for their own occupation, which stood in stark contrast to the makeshift slums and hovels of the urban poor.

But the principles of housing supply began to change in the 1630s with the signal event in the commodification of homes: the granting of government permission for the development of two new residential squares in London, one at Covent Garden, the other at Lincoln's Inn Fields (by a twist of fate, the first house to be built on Lincoln's Inn Fields is now the office premises of the barristers' chambers where I work). In both cases, the landowners succeeded in petitioning King Charles I for lawful permission to produce a small district of modern houses not for themselves, nor even for anyone in particular, but for the sole purpose of selling them for profit. In other words, the houses were produced for exchange – they were commodities – and that process was now sanctioned by law. Both projects were successful enough, despite the interruption of the Civil War. And that success was enhanced by the return of the monarchy in 1660, which arrived with new ideas from the continent on how the super-rich might live. These early experiments in high living sparked a spree of urban property development and speculation that has never really stopped.

With the invention and legalisation of the housing commodity, of course, came the first conscientious objectors to commodification: the early-modern NIMBY. A 1645 petition presented to parliament against the Lincoln's Inn Fields development complained that the landowner had built the houses 'for his owne private lucre'.[3] But this objection was in vain. The seventeenth century marked the end of landlords and property developers being hauled before the Star Chamber for trial and punishment; old royal proclamations against housebuilding carried increasingly little weight, and urban development began in earnest.

From about 1660 onwards, the profitable experiments at Covent Garden and Lincoln's Inn Fields were replicated on a larger scale. It was also at this moment, under the Tenures Abolition Act of 1660, also known as the Statute of Tenures, that parliament abolished the various ancient service-based forms of rent that had persisted throughout feudalism, replacing them with a more standardised and straightforwardly financial obligation payable by tenants to landowners. The aim of the statute was to do away with the king's right to raise funds through feudal obligations, bypassing the need for parliamentary taxation, Charles I's abuse of which had been one of the proximate causes of the Civil War.

With this parliamentarian reform, a modern system of for-profit development began to take shape on former manorial lands, and speculation began to take hold. There were even attempts in the late seventeenth century to fund government spending by raising money based on the resulting increases in land values. The new model of housing production typically involved an urban square being laid out, sometimes with a small market to compensate for the distance from the established city, and the homes around it being marketed to the highest-possible calibre of householder. The proceeds from the sales then financed the construction of the developer's own grand home on the site. Number 10 Downing Street itself – now the seat of the British government – was part of a speculative scheme of the 1680s built by the property developer and Civil War turncoat Sir John Downing. Eventually the middling sort were incorporated, too, some schemes making specific provision for humbler new houses in the back- and side-streets, while some entire projects were aimed at a slightly poorer class of resident.

Once again, the law played a central role in ensuring the profitability of these projects. The manorial lands to the north and west of London – in places like Knightsbridge, Mayfair and Bloomsbury – were viable for development because their ownership tended to be structured through a still-recognisable system of 'freehold' and 'leasehold'. Leasehold was a medieval innovation that had in effect led to the invention of the very concept of the landlord: a leasehold was, as it remains, a legally recognised and protected right that allowed its owner (the tenant) to make use of the land while the freeholder (landlord) was able to exploit the profits at one remove. By the seventeenth century, this well-established system had evolved to allow landowners to grant building leases, so that the financial risks of building could be passed down the chain to property developers, while the landowner's investment matured over time.

At the same time, however, London's eastern suburbs – such as the manors of Stepney and Hackney – were held under a semi-feudal 'copyhold' system of short leases that incorporated an ungodly jumble of local customary obligations. This did not lend itself to profiting from the slow process of building expensive, permanent structures and speculating on future ground rents, and so early developers had little interest in eastward expansion. Other factors, such as the prevailing winds blowing the city's stench eastwards, also meant that developers in the east could hardly boast to potential buyers about the high status of the neighbourhood, despite the area's flourishing shipbuilding and trade activities.

So, while the capital in this period was bursting at the seams in its efforts to house the oversized population that had been crammed within and around its walls since Tudor times, legal irregularities meant that land values and property development were unevenly distributed. But it was this method of property development – sub-letting land to produce and sell homes in order to maximise its underlying rentable value – that has shaped our built environment and living conditions ever since.

Over the following decades and centuries, Britain – particularly England, and even more particularly London – underwent capitalist development sooner and more rapidly than its peers. London had exploded to become Europe's largest city, and by the mid nineteenth century England's proportion of city-dwellers (more than 40 per cent) dwarfed that of France (14.4 per cent) and Germany (10.8 per cent).[4] This massive urban population was a very significant new source of rental income: just as early capitalism was characterised by new markets for cheap consumer goods as the new working class took shape, London and other cities saw the emergence of an important new market for bad housing. Wage labourers were compelled to become consumers of homes, and this fact shaped the development of newly emerging property rights and practices.

Victorian Discoveries

'In most great towns, in the 1830s or 1840s', wrote E. P. Thompson, 'doctors and sanitary reformers, Benthamites and Chartists, fought repeated battles for improvement against the inertia of property-owners and the demagoguery of "cheap government" rate-payers.'[5] The perpetual failure of such calls for improvement led to anxious debates around the underlying 'land question', which increasingly tended to focus on the new urban forms of property ownership that had emerged as cities grew in size and importance.

In the Victorian era, housing profits were no longer the exclusive preserve of pedigreed manor-holders and their contractors. Instead, there was a growing phenomenon of petty entrepreneurs exploiting leases and sub-tenancies for profit. While this had begun in the previous centuries, many of the non-landowners profiting from development had been investment-builders by trade (typified by Nicholas Barbon), rather than residential landlords. It was not until the nineteenth century that a sophisticated system emerged of rent extraction by a class of middlemen who did not themselves own the land. Housing in the nineteenth century 'reached the ultimate consumer, often enough, only through a maze of intermediate leases and subleases between the ground landlord and the tenant'.[6] The Victorians had discovered a new profession: that of the rentier.

By the 1870s – just as in the aftermath of the 2008 financial crisis – poor performance on world commodity markets meant that rack-renting the urban working class was a good bet for the small investor looking for business opportunities.[7] This approach was intended purely to maximise extraction, rather than – in the style of the aristocratic manor owners and their agents – to balance the competing social and economic demands of communities, albeit with a weather eye on longer-term profits. Many urban Victorian landlords were not freeholders, or even leaseholders, but a variety of middle-men who crammed hard-working families into insalubrious buildings and charged as much as they could. Some were former tradespeople seeking a more genteel source of income in their later years. Others were simple crooks messing around with the 'tail-ends' of expiring leases and assigning ownership to workhouse inmates to avoid liability for repairs.

An obscure but fascinating book that seeks to blame lawyers for obstructing land reform – due to their vested interest in maintaining the extravagant fees chargeable when systems have maximal complexity – economic historian Avner Offer has shown that, during the second half of the nineteenth century, the national rent bill paid to landowners *fell* fairly significantly (from about £44 million to £37 million). But rental receipts ballooned in respect of the housing that was sitting on their land: from about £48 million to £163 million over the same period.[8] Offer estimates that there were about a million 'small-fry' leasehold capitalists in the late nineteenth century: non-owners who had taken to sub-letting small parcels of urban space for as much rent as their tenants could muster.[9]

This vast proliferation of these individual entrepreneurs in the era of joint stock companies was probably partly due to 'mortmain', an ancient legal principle that prohibited corporations from obtaining land, as they would never pass it on through death and inheritance. Mortmain had been established under thirteenth- and sixteenth-century statutes, and was aimed at preventing the monasteries from owning land in perpetuity. The laws prevented corporations from owning land without a royal licence, and remained in force (and largely intact) until the very end of the nineteenth century. So while the railway developers, international trading houses and all sorts of industrialists were making use of the risk-reducing effects of company structures, land tended to be owned by natural persons. The archetype of the Victorian slum-lord is therefore derived from the very real physical presence of such people in their tenants' lives.

The Victorian private rented sector – which was wholly unregulated in terms of rent, and very sparsely regulated in terms of squalor – saw landlords achieving profit margins of over 25 per cent, as the constant threat of eviction allowed them to eat ever-further into their tenants' wages.[10] This will no doubt sound familiar from the description of the current system already set out, or indeed to anyone who has lived in rented housing in recent years. While the underlying land itself was still owned by the generationally wealthy, the real business of the Victorian era was the profit made by middle-class rentiers with mere tenurial interests.

The housing crisis that then unfolded in the 1880s provided a sandbox for experimentation with unchecked rental markets in which landlords were free to exhaust the means of the working class: rapidly rising rents, particularly in overcrowded areas, led to many poorer households paying between a third and a half of their incomes on poor-quality accommodation.[11] This process was taking place precisely while Marx was writing about the tendency of urban rents to reach monopoly prices.

At the same time, a significant number of new developments in the suburbs, as well as some 'model dwellings' in city centres (early forms of social housing), both lay empty, as their relatively higher prices forced tenants to cling to the overcrowded rookeries. Then, as now, the mere existence of plenty of housing was an inadequate tonic for the ills that occur when landlords are free to find the limits of people's means. The state's attempts to deal with the resulting slums played straight into the landlords' hands: the generous remuneration for slum demolitions was based on the rentable value of the land, which induced many landlords to exaggerate or even intensify their overcrowding and rack-renting activities.

During this period, before the twentieth-century municipalism movement took root in housing, there were a large number of charitable projects for improving working-class housing. Successful schemes included rather patrician projects like that of Octavia Hill, whose method of 'bettering' the working class through the ministrations of specially hired lady rent collectors and repeated threats of eviction for defaulting tenants meant that properties under her stewardship were coaxed into yielding their 5 per cent profit margin. While Hill's schemes were a vast improvement on other charitable working-class housing projects, and while she tended to advocate redeveloping house-by-house to avoid the mass displacements caused by slum clearances, her methods were incapable of solving the broad problem of adequately housing a population that was casually employed and badly paid. Instead, its successes were limited to helping the restricted number of 'respectable' working tenants whose wages allowed them to comply with Hill's edicts on household economics. Charity could not cure poverty on such a large scale.

Shortly after the great housing crisis of the 1880s, there followed another, just as severe but entirely different in form. The 1880s had seen badly paid tenants paying well over the odds to live in squalor while there was plenty of housing to go around, simply because landlords could charge whatever they wanted. But the crisis in 1898–1902 was founded on a boom rather than on hardship. High employment and buoyant wages were causing many households to abandon cramped, shared accommodation and look for somewhere of their own. They sought to escape the overcrowded tenements, or to upgrade their living situations in various other ways, but by this point there was simply not enough housing to go around.[12]

The Fabians published a tract with the entirely appropriate name of *The Housing Famine and How to Relieve It*. It contains exactly the sort of commentary many would tend to reproduce today – though that reflects an ignorance of the fact that the present crisis is not of the 1900-type, but is instead similar to 1885: an adequate number of homes exist, but they are too expensive for many people to access under the economic circumstances of the day. It is very difficult to cast the 2020s as a 1900-style crisis of generalised affluence and housing shortage after more than a decade of stagnating wages and austerity, and an ever-increasing ratio of dwellings to households.

As Victorian tract development had expanded with the railways, ancient systems of landownership had become inappropriate to society's needs. The nineteenth century saw the gradual erosion and replacement of the vestiges of manorial landownership, under which a tangle of ancient and undiscernible rights and duties had been attached to individual parcels of land. In 1832, law reformers complained of the copyhold system that 'Each manor has for itself a system of laws to be sought in oral traditions, or in the court rolls or proceedings of the customary court, kept often by ignorant or negligent stewards.'[13] This was not conducive to the swift and easy commodification of new housing sites, and various acts of parliament sought to phase the copyhold system out – for the benefit of property speculators. Freehold and leasehold offered much more fertile soil in which the seeds sown by housing developers could grow as the land surrounding industrialising towns and cities shot up in value. Thus, the replacement of customary obligations with market-based economic rents saw ever more land subsumed under capitalist principles. The result was the boom in the 'developer Victorian' style of architecture (often now repurposed for marketing reasons as 'period' architecture) that still makes up such a great deal of the national housing stock.

However, debates about broader aspects of land reform ebbed and flowed throughout the nineteenth century to little avail. Calls for the formal abolition of primogeniture – by which the ultimate ownership of land was passed down through the male first-born – and the replacement of complex deed-searching processes with a simple registration system were consistently defeated. This is why the Victorian petty entrepreneurs had had to resort to trading in tenurial rights over land in the first place, rather than in the land itself: they simply could not secure outright ownership. But their caucus became a steadily more powerful one over the course of the nineteenth century, as leaseholders sought to pursue their own policies against more aristocratic interests. They wanted to make it easier to buy and sell property rights ('free trade in land'), and sought a legal right to convert their leasehold interests into freehold ones.

This was a dilemma for the landowning class. On the one hand, the petty housing rentiers were a protective force against revolution: an acceptable dilution of the concentration of landed property ownership that had caused such upheaval across Europe. On the other, strengthening the rights of leaseholders and petty landlords represented a direct encroachment on the freeholders' own property rights.

In the 1880s there was an attempt to unite the interests of leaseholding landlords with those of freeholder aristocrats. Their 'Liberty and Property Defence League' was specifically billed as an anti-socialist project. But it did not succeed: there was an irreconcilable conflict of interest between the two camps, and the aristocrats' standpoint was in fact supported by some radical reformers who saw leasehold reform as a retrograde step. By degrees, however, the system of leasehold rentierism ultimately became more secure, formal and valuable in its own right. It matured from a Victorian hustle into the regularised basis of landholding and rent-extraction that we see today.

Leasehold remained the driving force behind acts of creative destruction throughout the nineteenth century: when long leases expired, the land reverted back to the freeholder. The freeholder then tended to knock everything down and redevelop the land, which was a major problem for both the leaseholder (who was removed from the picture entirely at the end of the lease) and the occupiers (who were forced out when their homes were destroyed). While an 1884 Royal Commission for the Housing of the Working Classes called for leasehold reform as a means of improving the housing situation, it was not until the twentieth century that lease-hold owners won the legal right to extend leases or compulsorily purchase the freehold.

Bizarrely, this legislation led to a legal challenge brought by the Duke of Westminster, who took a case to the European Court of Human Rights arguing that the forced sale of housing on his land in Belgravia to its leasehold owners was a breach of his right to respect for property. The Duke lost in Strasbourg, and the domes-tic law on leasehold enfranchisement still stands.

British capitalism evolved not by expropriating land from aristo-cratic interests, but by increasing the relative power and extractive capacity of subsidiary and tenurial interests. The land law devel-opments of the nineteenth century, as Joseph Chamberlain complained, were 'tainted and paralysed by the incurable timidity with which Parliament, largely recruited from men of great posses-sions, is accustomed to deal with the sacred rights of property'; but the definition of 'property' had expanded well beyond mere own-ership of the land itself. It now meant leases: owning the houses, owning control over the land, having the right to exploit people's need for land.[14] The Victorian framework of land and housing was capitalist par excellence.

Abolish Landlords (Again)

During the 1970s a consensus emerged that the private rented sector was dying. Between 1972 and 1973 alone, privately let homes fell from 16 per cent of dwellings to 13 per cent, having stood at 61 per cent at the end of the Second World War. It seemed inevitable that the downward trajectory would not just continue, but accelerate.

The story of social housing is now relatively well known. In the first half of the twentieth century the Victorian dread of state-funded housing was overcome, municipal socialism emerged, and a political consensus was eventually reached among politicians of all stripes, who fell over themselves to promise more council homes.

It is important not to be misty-eyed about the heyday of social housing, and to acknowledge its imperfections even when looking back at it from the apocalyptic environment of the present. Equally, however, it is difficult to overstate the significance of mid-century housing policies for the political economy of land. The taking of large amounts of urban land into public control, and the removal of millions of people from private renting, was a hugely significant achievement. David Madden and Peter Marcuse describe the 'partially decommodified character' of twentieth-century housing policy, under which housing was 'established as a social right, and state-owned housing sectors accounted for most or all residential growth'. Slum-clearance schemes and the enforcement of obligations to provide social housing for the homeless made the Dickensian era seem ever more distant.

But perhaps the most important aspect of the mid-century decommodification project was the near-death of private landlordism itself. While it is often pointed out that the private rented sector was much smaller before Thatcher came to power, what tends to be forgotten is just how close we came to abolishing landlordism altogether, and just how recently. The knock-on effect of this partial decommodification was to break the economic power of rent-seekers and land speculators, who almost did not recover from the shock.

In 1973 a group of social-democratic lawyers wrote a Fabian pamphlet called *The End of the Private Landlord*, and the right immediately nodded in agreement. The following year, the Conservative

Political Centre (CPC) published *The Eclipse of the Private Landlord: A Study of the Consequences*. The theme was then taken up in the press, with death notices appearing in *The Times* ('Decline and Fall of the Landlord', John Brennan, 1976) and *New Society* ('Landlords' Slow Goodbye', David Eversley, 1975). Even the Institute of Economic Affairs, in a 1972 pamphlet co-edited by Friedrich Hayek and Milton Friedman, took the view that 'the present system will result in the gradual withdrawal from the letting market of all privately-owned houses suitable for owner-occupancy'.[15]

As interest rates reached 12 per cent and rent controls ensured ever-smaller yields, landlordism made little financial sense. Regulatory changes were making it less lucrative to let out cheaper homes than more expensive ones, and many of those who could not cater to the small class of better-heeled tenants were selling up entirely. With Labour councils championing the further expansion of social housing, on the one hand, while Tory governments privileged homeownership policies (such as tax breaks and the building society movement) on the other, both parties' philosophies tended towards curbing private lettings. The result was that rentiers had few political friends. Landlords were fleeing in droves, and it was genuinely thought that they would reach extinction. By 1979 private letting had dwindled even further, to just 7 per cent of dwellings; there were about half as many private tenants as six years earlier.

The Fabians' standpoint was that a small private sector might usefully be retained as a 'safety valve' for young people leaving home and workers moving around to follow job prospects, but it is interesting that they felt compelled to come up with a defence at all. Their broader argument was that sustaining a private rented sector even as it existed in the 1970s was not only socially and economically indefensible, but politically impossible even for a Conservative government.

Indeed, the CPC's own view was that 'the accelerating decline of the privately-rented sector is quite irreversible. The private

landlord, as he exists now and has existed, will, within a generation, be almost as extinct as the dinosaur. There is nothing that can
be done about this.' They viewed 'the dying private-letting sector'
not as any great tragedy, but as a simple fact of life. Many Conservatives seem to have recognised the benign, popular effects of driving
out landlordism, and wanted renters' conditions to improve. Tories
in the 1970s merely sought to retain a small number of petty landlords, who ought to be entitled to a 'fair return' if they let out a few
spare rooms.[16]

Today, the merest hint of reducing the massive private rented
sector is met with a mixture of derision and alarm. When we hear
horror stories about landlords having to sell up, and the world-
ending consequences that would surely follow, it is useful to
remember that the process went well enough last time round, at
least in terms of housing outcomes.

There was a powerful constituency in favour of 'municipalisation', whereby distressed landlords were encouraged to sell to local
authorities that would take over the tenancies as council housing.
With landlords desperate to sell, and councils having access to
preferential loan arrangements and grants, there was not even a
need for compulsory purchase, and social housing stocks were able
to grow cheaply, sustainably, and without a single new brick being
laid. In the early 1970s the Wilson government issued a circular
encouraging municipalisation, Denis Healey made £200 million
available in the budget, and a 'good sensible Socialist Government'
criticised the Conservatives because *their* criteria for municipalisation purchases under Heath had been too generous: 'almost a *carte
blanche*', complained Labour's minister for the environment.[17]

In 1973 and 1974 alone, Camden Council municipalised more
than 4,000 privately rented homes through voluntary sales, which
represented about 10 per cent of the borough's entire private rented
sector.[18] A contemporaneous article proposed municipalism as a
route towards 'the end of landlordism in London . . . With

commitment it could be achieved in six years – it would be easy to do in ten.'[19] And there was a Tory-friendly counterpart to this policy: many homes were bought by their current tenants. A shrinking private sector was good news all round.

Our recent history shows us that landlord abolition is an entirely realistic ambition. In fact, it is so modest a demand that it has been comfortably subsumed into Conservative Party policy.

Indeed, when we come across opponents of rent controls, it is worth considering that, by twentieth-century standards, it is they who would have been the ones with outlandish policy demands – the extremists, the profiteers, the landlord apologists, who believed in an economy that involved skimming as much passive income from people's wages as was humanly possible. If they do not believe in rent controls, they believe that rents should be set by the market, which (in the context of urban housing) tends to mean monopoly prices. They believe in a mechanism that necessitates poverty, and by which the already-wealthy thrive on other people's money. By anyone else's standards, the world is better off without landlords.

The mid 1970s was a critical moment, when the fate of private renting hung in the balance. But as close as we came to the death of the private landlord, we never held up a mirror to that hungry maw to check that it had breathed its last. It did not die completely, and – as Chapter 3 will explore – landlordism was nursed back into life, and then into rude health, over the next few decades. The Conservatives had begun to pursue the idea of 'shorthold' tenancies within months of Thatcher becoming leader of the opposition in 1975. At the time it seemed to them to be a fairly benign policy, designed to make it easier to let empty inner-city flats. But that was because it was originally supposed to operate in a context of rent controls, and in combination with a steady increase in the amount of council housing.[20] It was as that surrounding policy environment fundamentally changed over the next few decades that shorthold tenure took on its socially devastating character.

Neoliberal Longevity

In a secret Cabinet memorandum written in 1963, Enoch Powell set out his belief that the government ought to play a very limited role in housing provision. Central government, he recognised, laid no bricks; but in his view the task of the state ought merely to be to control some of the economic impetuses that result in housebuilding. 'Within limits', he said 'we can cajole them into building more.'[21]

This view was unorthodox in the heyday of council-house building, during a period of consensus in favour of the price-suppressing effects of rent controls. But by the start of the 1980s it had become foundational to government thinking, and has remained with us ever since. A high-profile 1985 Parliamentary Inquiry into British Housing concluded that physical conditions were poor, and that it was crucial that private capital be attracted into the sector – mainly by boosting the private rented sector. Housing was now all about supply, and the role of the state was merely to cajole builders by ensuring that it would be profitable to produce new homes.

This is the lens through which the state now tends to see the housing crisis, and the focus of its attempts to resolve it. The state is not concerned so much with the direct *production* of housing as with its *circulation*: its measures are aimed at tinkering with price, with the ultimate aim of incentivising builders and mortgage lenders. Successive governments have tended to pursue policies that ensure a buoyant and profitable private rental market – and, more recently, policies aimed at ensuring that first-time buyers can meet the ever-rising costs of homeownership. The ideological switch that took place under Thatcher has never been reversed, or even interrupted. Tragically, in 2022, former housing minister Gavin Barwell admitted to a public inquiry that the government's housing supply agenda had even overshadowed 'life critical' fire safety works before the Grenfell fire.[22]

This enduring cross-party consensus has had a profound negative impact on the political economy of housing. The reason why the Conservative Political Centre had been so convinced that the decline of the private landlord in the 1970s was irreversible was their realisation that, even if landlord-friendly policies were imposed while the Conservatives were in office, no one would bother to invest in land because it was inevitable that Labour would periodically come along and reverse them again. National Labour administrations throughout the twentieth century had tended to tighten up rent controls, while local administrations continually pursued the provision of public housing at the expense of the private rented sector. Land is a long-term investment, and it is not an attractive one when these threats and interruptions loom constantly in the background. 'One does not allow one's best china in a kitchen', the CPC explained in characteristically snobbish terms, 'where the most careful dishwasher is occasionally replaced by one who throws the plates about.'[23]

By that logic, the Blair and Brown governments imposed an extraordinary amount of harm. They did nothing to oppose the reanimation of the private rented sector under Thatcher and Major, but instead demonstrated to land speculators that there was no longer any need to be shy about investing. Rent controls were not coming back, even when Labour won landslide elections. Council housing was prised from the inefficient hands of local government, rather than expanded, as the social sector became dominated by housing associations and 'arm's-length management organisations'. As a result, the pro-tenant attitude that had kept land speculators in check *even during periods of Conservative power* ultimately evaporated.

A timid Labour Party, whether in office or in opposition, is a dangerous thing: its mere ideological posture can have tangible effects. In that sense, the misery of the current housing crisis owes as much to Blair and Brown as it does to Thatcher. They broke the state's grip on landlords and house-price speculators, as it became clear that there was no longer anything to fear from governments of either stripe. The era of the 'partial decommodification' of land – and the profound economic effects that went with it – was finished.

The deregulation of the private rented sector lifted the lid on a buoyant housing market that had been artificially constrained for decades. The phasing-out of rent controls and the gradual withdrawal of social housing reintroduced an essentially Victorian environment in which rentiers and speculators were again free to explore the limits of tenants' means. Not much has changed about the physical environment – we continue to live in many of the exact same buildings; but the cost of occupying those homes has skyrocketed. And while an unfathomable amount of government policy has been introduced and mooted in the intervening decades, none of it begins to challenge the logic of 'full commodification'. Everything is focused on the circulation of housing: keeping prices as high as possible as an indirect means of procuring new homes. But this necessarily involves maintaining the profitability of land, and therefore none of these policies has been able to work.

Perhaps the most extreme example of this type of thinking is John Prescott's 'Pathfinder' project, launched in 2003. In a scheme calculated to give economists bad dreams, the idea was that the government might tackle 'failing housing markets' by refurbishing – or even demolishing and rebuilding – homes in areas where nobody wanted to live. This, it was thought, might revive flagging areas and regions. But even the earliest capitalists knew that demand for housing sites is driven by their proximity to prosperity, and not the other way around. Some of the very areas of the Midlands where the Pathfinder scheme was implemented had provided the first demonstrations of that fact, as the land around places like Birmingham shot up in value as nearby towns and cities industrialised. New Labour seemed to think not only that the tail could wag the dog, but that rising housing costs were an unambiguously worthy objective.[24]

Pathfinder ground to a halt with the global financial crisis, but its spectre returned in 2012 in the form of Nick Clegg's £1 billion 'Kickstart' scheme to bail out property developers whose projects had been mothballed during the recession. The bulk of the homes funded would be developed for profit, rather than meeting the increasingly tortured definition of 'affordable'. While much of the funding was in the form of loans or equity financing, millions of pounds was simply handed to private developers.

Similarly hare-brained was the coalition government's £10 billion housing guarantee of 2013. This involved the government giving out preferential loans to property developers so that they could build new privately rented housing.[25] This was perhaps the nadir of British housing policy: instead of the Thatcherite method of encouraging landlordism through deregulation, and then indirectly funding it through Housing Benefit, the state decided to pass money directly to institutional landlords.

Thatcher's Children, Blair's Renters

One of the joys of being a tenants' rights lawyer – at least when landlords do not send belligerent QCs to hassle me – is turning up to court and watching the colour drain from a landlord's face as I explain that there is a defence to the eviction claim, and the landlord realises that they might not win. The state has *promised* landlords that they can evict people quickly, easily and cheaply, but sometimes they find out that section 21 is a qualified promise.

A range of technical defences are available. Where landlords have broken the law in terms of deposit protection, or informing tenants about some of their rights, or providing information about gas safety or energy performance, or a range of other issues, the law sometimes allows tenants to defeat the claim. In many ways this is a bizarre means of protecting tenants; it simply delays evictions and annoys landlords. But there is a circuitous logic to these technical defences.

It is emblematic of neoliberalism that no one is 'in charge' of standards in the private rented sector. After years of de-funding, local authorities are unlikely to use their inspection and enforcement powers because they no longer have the resources. In 2022, a BBC investigation found that councils in England had only taken, on average, 5,000 enforcement actions each year, when almost 20 per cent of privately rented homes are thought to be in a hazardous condition.[26] Realistically, there is no state authority that tenants can call when something is wrong with their home. Responsibility for policing housing standards has been shifted to the tenants themselves.

But tenants are in a pitifully weak position. Many tenants know that it is folly to challenge a landlord over repairs or conditions given the high risk of an eviction. The mechanism that parliament has come up with is therefore to try to give tenants at least some clout by hitting the landlord where it hurts: the eviction process. Unless a landlord has complied with the law – and notably this only applies to a select number of laws – they are not allowed to evict, and they are stuck with the tenant until they comply. By this strange method, vitally important issues like gas safety are litigated by means of a technicality in an eviction claim.

The same goes for the duty to provide details about energy performance, which – under current circumstances – can constitute life-altering financial information. We now find ourselves at the logical dead-end of the Thatcherite reforms to the private rented sector, whose resurgence was supposed to result in a greater supply specifically of high-quality homes. Insisting on decent standards in the private rented sector has turned out to be a a fool's errand.

Meanwhile, as the post-Thatcher governments have spent increasingly lavish amounts of money on minimising the financial risks of speculative landownership, the housing crisis has come inexorably to the boil. Housing costs have risen with property values, becoming ever more unaffordable, while stocks of available social housing have dwindled.

One of the best indicators of the state of the housing crisis is homelessness policy. Over the decades, governments gradually came to realise that they could no longer realistically require local authorities to comply with legal obligations dating back to the 1970s to provide council housing where they had a duty to rehouse homeless people. In 2008 the government began to allow councils to give people the option of either accepting a private-sector tenancy or waiting for a social tenancy – and in 2011 another change removed the obligation to offer social housing at all. Whereas councils had formerly been obliged to accommodate people in cheap, secure council housing, a gradual assault on the rights of the homeless means that the most that can be hoped for now is a perversely expensive, insecure home in the private sector – paid for, of course, by the state itself.

But as this crisis has unfolded, the state has done everything possible to solve it except for attacking the very system of rentierism that is its fundamental cause. Governments will adjust stamp duty or encourage mortgage lending, devise special schemes for first-time buyers or cajole the building industry, but discussing the policy approach that prevailed until the 1970s will not be countenanced.

In a speech to the 2022 Labour Party conference, the shadow housing minister said, 'Housing isn't a market. It's a fundamental human right.' As a statement of fact, this could not be further from the truth. Housing has been a market for hundreds of years. Generations of homeless and badly housed people would testify against any claim that it is a human right. Over the course of the last 500 years, residential landlordism was invented, finessed, nearly destroyed, and finally championed by the state. Housing was made subject to market forces centuries ago, although the extent of its commodification has waxed and waned. To anyone who had understood the emergence of rentierism in the nineteenth century, today's woes would have seemed inevitable: an economy predicated on maximising rent-extraction will naturally tend towards disaster – but that is exactly the policy the state has pursued since the 1980s. This is a crisis by design.

3

The Making of the English Landlord Class

Poor people's houses seldom belong to any but those who are glad to get any money they can; they belong to a little shopkeeping class of persons . . . I think very few persons of great capital have anything to do with them at all.

Thomas Cubitt, evidence to the Select Committee
on the Health of Towns

There is often a nerve-wracking moment in court when a tenant tries to defend against an eviction for rent arrears by raising a disrepair counterclaim. Depending on the size of the tenant's debt and the viability or seriousness of the disrepair claim, the judge can either allow the tenant to argue their case to trial, or grant the landlord's claim and order the tenant to leave their home. There are cases that could go either way: court hearings in which my body tenses, my voice feels like it is starting to strain, and I resort to looking straight into the judge's eyes, refusing to blink until the judge does. We walk away, my client and I, keyed up and hyperalert, to discuss the outcome.

When I represented Gail at her eviction hearing, though, my nerves were perfectly steady. The debt was relatively small – a few hundred pounds of unpaid utility bills – but more importantly the disrepair was dreadful. I sat calmly while the judge glanced through a surveyor's report. 'Your client has no working heating *at all*?' he asked me. It was true. The judge was, quite rightly, genuinely shocked by the fact that Gail had to heat her studio flat by leaving the oven door open; but the heating had never worked during the two years that she had lived there, and that was all she could do. It was, of course, incredibly dangerous to do this when her small children came to stay with her, so they would struggle in the cold. At least, that is, until her landlord sent her a devastating letter notifying her that a change in the 'house rules' meant her children were prohibited from staying the night.

What made Gail's case striking, though, was not the squalor, nor even the meanness of the landlord. It is a sad fact that housing conditions and petty-minded interferences are a fact of life in the private rented sector. Instead, it was the fact that Gail's landlord was the well-known homelessness charity St Mungo's.

St Mungo's has been helping homeless people for more than fifty years. It started out by providing practical assistance to people who were sleeping rough, and quickly – and admirably – moved on to providing the thing that they needed: accommodation. But as time went on, the charity seems to have realised that its role as a landlord was an impressive source of income. A 2016 'value for money self-assessment' explained that St Mungo's delivered its 'objectives as a housing association and a homelessness charity by operating a business model that combines a landlord function, with the delivery of commissioned service contracts, and fundraised income'. The figures showed just how profitable that landlord function had become. The charity's rental receipts were three times as high as its fundraising income. While the bulk of this rental income appeared to be government-funded payments for providing supported housing, which is not so objectionable, St Mungo's also openly operates in the 'real lettings' sector: in other words, as a garden-variety private landlord.

This was reflected in the behaviour of the charity's 'rent service partner' – the staff member who argued for Gail's eviction at the court hearing. He said that our surveyor's report and intention to raise a counterclaim for damages was 'a bit over the top', until I pointed out that St Mungo's was seeking to make Gail homeless over a small amount in unpaid utility bills. It was exactly the kind of banal cruelty that characterises so many private landlords' behaviour: the logic of 'I just want my property back', without regard to the human drama that this necessarily sets in motion.

The example of St Mungo's shows that the phenomenon of landlordism has become so widespread, so apparently benign and socially acceptable, that even a homelessness charity does not see the irony in operating as a real-estate profiteer during a housing crisis.

This is, to an extent, nothing new. In Victorian Britain there was a strain of housing assistance schemes known as '5 per cent philanthropy' or 'charity at 5 per cent'. It was so-called because its financial backers, rather than being mere benefactors, were lending to charitable projects that built housing for the 'labouring poor' with a guaranteed rate of return – to 'reward the pocket as well as the conscience', as historian John Burnett puts it.[1] Then, as now, working-class housing tended to pay for itself (and then some, as the Marx quote at the beginning of this book indicates). Bearing that in mind, the purpose of this chapter is to look at the peculiarities of the landlord class in Britain – a vast but disparate group of 'respectable' petty-bourgeois individuals – and to explain how it developed, and what its continuing existence means.

The English Landlord Class

HMRC estimates that there are more than 2.5 million landlords in the country.[2] That means that roughly one in every twenty-six people is a landlord, or one in every twenty-one adults. There are four times as many landlords as teachers. There are nearly twice as many landlords as there are employees of NHS England – the

country's largest employer. When I was born, at the tail-end of the
Thatcher years, there were about 600,000, which means that an
additional 2 million landlords have been created over the course of
my lifetime.[3] They walk among us and, frankly, it is difficult not to
think of the urban myth that you are never more than six feet away
from a rat in the city. How has this happened?

Theodor Adorno said: 'The theorist who intervenes in practical
controversies nowadays discovers on a regular basis and to his
shame that whatever ideas he might contribute were expressed
long ago – and usually better the first time around.'[4] Anyone who
has ever written about the ideological reasons behind the project of
a 'property-owning democracy' – and there have been many –
would have done well to look at Engels's *The Housing Question*,
which cites a wonderfully prescient and astute passage from a
Spanish newspaper, *La Emancipación*, published in 1872:

> The cleverest leaders of the ruling class have always directed their
> efforts towards increasing the number of small property owners in
> order to build an army for themselves against the proletariat. The
> bourgeois revolutions of the last century divided up the big estates of
> the nobility and the church into small allotments, just as the Spanish
> republicans propose to do today with the still existing large estates,
> and created thereby a class of small landowners which has since
> become the most reactionary element in society and a permanent
> hindrance to the revolutionary movement of the urban proletariat.
> Napoleon III aimed at creating a similar class in the towns by reduc-
> ing the denominations of the individual bonds of the public debt, and
> M. Dollfus and his colleagues sought to stifle all revolutionary spirit
> in their workers by selling them small dwellings to be paid for in
> annual instalments, and at the same time to chain the workers by this
> property to the factory once they worked in it. Thus the Proudhon
> plan, far from bringing the working class any relief, even turned
> directly against it.[5]

But we can trace this ideology further back, beyond the French Revolution, to the advice of the Board of Trade to King George III in 1764. The Board said that, by granting property rights, the state could mollify the existing French colonial inhabitants of the newly British colonies of St Vincent and Dominica. Fearful of losing the labour of the 10,000 people whom the 3,000 French citizens were keeping enslaved on the islands, the Board recommended granting the colonists leases on their existing land (recognisable under newly imposed British laws) rather than dispossessing them. They assuaged the king's worry about security risks from 'Our natural Rivals the French' by pointing out that 'experience shews, that the possession of property is the best Security for a due obedience and submission to Government'.[6]

This analysis is thus much older than the coining of the term 'property-owning democracy' by Tory MP Noel Skelton in the *Spectator* in 1923. It long pre-dates the arguments that many current thinkers have made about the ideological function of homeownership under Thatcherism. But the more modern approaches are also worth examining.

David Harvey claims that the great social prestige that attaches to homeownership has been actively fostered, and that the expansion of homeownership into the middle and working classes has been facilitated because it 'performs an ideological and legitimizing function for all forms of private property'.[7] This view has been accepted even among some of Harvey's sharpest critics.[8] The idea, which reached new heights under Thatcherism, is that admitting a greater number of people into the club of landownership convinces them of the need to preserve the sanctity of private property in general, and thus of capitalism more broadly.

But what was new about Thatcherism – what distinguished it from the ideology of the nineteenth and even the eighteenth century – was that it did not simply enhance the ordinary person's ability to own their own home, but also made it much easier to own other people's homes. When the Thatcher, Major and Blair governments rescued the private rented sector from its death throes, they did so by creating the conditions for a *multiple*-property-owning-democracy. They created a new cadre of millions of little rentiers – a whole class, a whole generation, of Thatcher's landlords.

Unlike in most wealthy countries, privately rented housing in Britain is overwhelmingly owned by individuals rather than corporate landlords. Data from the English Private Landlord Survey in 2021 showed that a full 94 per cent of landlords in England were private individuals rather than companies, almost half of them owning just one rented property, and a further 39 per cent owning four or fewer. The rental market is dominated by millions of small-time side-hustlers with an average age of fifty-eight, rather than by real-estate capital.

This is not to say that the private rented sector is not big business. On the contrary, it is estimated that a total of £63 billion was paid in rent in the UK in 2022, dwarfing industrial sectors like agriculture and pharmaceuticals.[9] This vast section of the national economy, instead of being governed by 'captains of industry' and high-level executives, is stewarded by more than 2.5 million individuals who are almost wholly unregulated by the state.

The peculiarly non-corporate nature of the contemporary British landlord class can be traced back to the post-war period. The first half of the twentieth century had seen a growth in corporate investment in land, as many of the aristocratic estates were broken up and sold off and as the old 'mortmain' restrictions fell away. By the 1960s, however, only about 36 per cent of privately rented housing in Greater London was company-owned (countrywide data is lacking), and this share had been steadily declining since the Second World War.

Since then, it has shrunk much further: in 2021, 13 per cent of tenancies in England were granted by corporate landlords – but many of these may have been individuals acting under a corporate identity. Some estimates put corporate landlordism proper at less than 1 per cent.[10] The post-war boom of the 1950s and 1960s saw a trend of corporate landlords shifting their investment from residential property into commercial property.

As we have seen, there were handsome profits to be made by redeveloping commercial sites in a bomb-damaged country on a deregulatory spree, while at the same time the strict residential rent controls and the political controversy that surrounded housing persuaded many larger companies to sell off their property empires. Large institutional landowners like the Church Commissioners also sold many of their homes because they were 'embarrassed' by their landlord function at the peak of post-Rachman outrage.[11]

The exodus of corporate landlords left rented housing – particularly working-class rented housing – scattered among individual, private hands. This situation has not lent itself to the sort of corporate landlordism seen in many other parts of the world: homes do not tend to be held in portfolios that can be bought and sold en bloc. During the second half of the twentieth century, most rented homes were built by local government, and some local authorities were actively engaged in an avowed project of 'wresting housing out of the hands of slum landlords'.[12]

Almost no new homes were built for the specific purpose of providing lower-income people with private rented accommodation in the post-war period, given the rent controls that prevailed until the very late 1980s – although some private homes were built for owner-occupation. In fact, returns on working-class renting were so poor at mid-century that one of the few corporate landlords that was building flats in London in the early 1960s redeveloped a mixed-use site in west London with the intention of selling the flats to the council at cost, and making a profit from the shops alone.[13] Throughout the twentieth century, landlordism (like landownership in general) was increasingly the preoccupation of individuals. Needless to say, this fact has shaped political and social attitudes towards the regulation of housing up to the present.

The Tories' response to the flight of corporate capital from the private rented sector after the war was the winding-down of rent controls in 1957. This move was characterised by a lack of what we might now call evidence-based policymaking. Tedious old canards about rent controls were thrown around. Some Tory MPs who sat on the housing committee openly spoke on behalf of landlord pressure groups, and the government made almost no attempt to obtain data or analysis.[14] The case that the Conservatives made to the public in the 1950s was that de-control might ultimately lead to *reduced* rents – notwithstanding the Conservative Research Department's analysis, which suggested that just 6.5 per cent of income was spent on rents at the time (read it and weep).[15] But, apart from a couple of zealous pro-landlord members of the Tories' hard-right 'Bow Group', the movement to liberalise the rental sector in the 1950s was mainly driven by a real concern that rents had become so impossibly low that landlords – by then, as we have seen, mostly individuals – could not afford to carry out repairs, and that housing conditions were declining as a result.

The 1964 Milner Holland Committee on the state of housing in London, commissioned by Keith Joseph in response to the Rachman scandal, reported that liberalising rent controls alone had not been capable of 'reviving' the private rented sector in the 1950s. The arrangements for taxing homeownership, which favoured owner-occupiers, had undermined the 1957 attempt to woo landlords by de-controlling rents, so deregulation had simply failed to work.[16] The 1957 policy was reversed in 1965, shortly after Labour came to power and rent controls were thus restored just around the time that the average-aged landlord of today was born.

When they tried again in the 1980s, the Conservatives therefore knew they had to make changes on a much broader front. No doubt they had also learned from their experience of wholesale deregulation in the commercial property sector in the 1950s.[17] It was certainly in this spirit that Thatcher set about remodelling the residential property framework. When the Tories rebuilt the private rental market from its single-digit percentage of dwellings in the late 1980s, they continued, rather than reversed, the post-war tradition of personal, as opposed to corporate, landownership. A new focus developed on rented housing as a source of household wealth.

Virtually everyone who bought property from the 1980s onwards, when the average-aged landlords of today would have been in their early twenties, saw the value of their asset rise dramatically, as residential land prices slipped the leash of the rent controls that had restrained them since the Second World War. This gave all homeowners a very useful source of stability and wealth as the country's economy radically changed under neo-liberalism: a steady source of passive income and asset growth compensated for an increasingly insecure jobs market and wage stagnation, and for the slow dismantling of pensions, social care and adequate welfare provision.[18]

This trend also formed part of a wider shift away from an industrial economy and towards an assets- and services-based one. Inspired by an ideology known as 'asset-based welfare', the principle was that the fruits of land speculation were not to be hoarded by a landed elite, but shared among a growing number of middle- and working-class homeowners.

Which is all well and good, except – assuming it is correct that rising land values are largely derived from the rentable value of property – the regime it presupposes is something of a zero-sum game. The whole system of inflating housing assets is predicated on the existence of a strong and profitable rented sector. There will always need to be a relatively large number of renters who not only fail to benefit from asset-based welfare, but whose rent pays (whether actually or notionally) for homeowners' rising wealth.

As Harold Wilson put it in 1963, 'if some people can make a killing of £1 million by an overnight sale of property someone has to pay for that £1 million – it does not come from nowhere. It is paid for, of course, by the tenants.'[19]

As we saw in Chapter 1, those who owned or bought property from the late 1980s onwards were the beneficiaries of the assured shorthold tenancy regime, which allows rents and house prices to rise extraordinarily quickly. These tenancies became the default setting through a law passed in 1996, and in that same year buy-to-let mortgages became available. The availability of this cheap credit to everyday people, with loans assessed on the rentable value of the property, maintained the situation that individuals with relatively little cash, rather than big real-estate companies, could continue to dominate the rental market. Buy-to-let mortgages grew quickly in popularity from 2000 onwards: over the next fifteen years, the number of privately rented homes grew by 125 per cent.[20]

As the seeds of a housing crisis, sown in the 1980s and 1990s, reached maturity, the world was rocked by the global financial crisis of 2007–08. While there was a significant dip in house prices – a brief interruption of the usual process of crisis development, rather than a US-style massive crash – a variety of measures were put in place to ensure that housing assets weathered the storm. Quantitative easing and very low interest rates ensured that housing was a relatively safe haven for capital investment, and money continued to pour in. The 'Help to Buy' scheme was ostensibly a form of assistance for first-time buyers, but in reality it merely served to keep house prices buoyant.

Benefits claimants, having had their total entitlements capped and their housing payments decoupled from the market rent, rose to the coalition government's belt-tightening challenge by dipping further into their own pockets to ensure that rents did not fall. Some, even government ministers, expected rents to decline in pace with benefits cuts, but rent payers rather selflessly put house prices before themselves.[21] As with comparable policies such as the 'bedroom tax' and the 'two-child limit', millions of people somehow found enough flexibility in their household finances to make ends meet despite increasingly difficult circumstances. This was, after all, a society in which constantly rising rents had taken on the appearance of a self-evident natural law.

In 2009, two-thirds of all bank lending was for residential mortgages: within a few months of the crash, house prices were one of the few parts of the economy that was functioning just as profitably as before.[22] In a world that seemed to have stopped turning, landlords and homeowners continued to do very well.

No doubt this cushioning of some voters' household finances gave the coalition government the space it needed to impose austerity. As David Madden and Peter Marcuse observe, in the US context, homeowning 'reduces the demand for state action, as rising house prices are seen as compensation for inefficient social services'.[23] The class of rentiers and property owners, which had swelled in number since the 1980s, thus gave the government leave to impose a great deal of harm on the working class.

Again, the old wisdom is worth repeating here, as we seem to have lost sight of ideas that were so clear to earlier generations. In a 1932 debate about rent control in the midst of the Great Depression, Independent Labour Party MP James Maxton pointed out that 'every other section in the community has been asked to make some sacrifice, and the Government ought to have asked it of those whose incomes are derived from house-owning'.[24] The years after 2008 were dominated by that same narrative of sacrifice – of austerity for the public good; but very few made the case that we should halt, reverse, or even limit a system of passive income and property speculation. Instead, serious efforts were made to sustain and increase the value of homes – efforts that were broadly effective. While Britain has never properly recovered from the global financial crisis (particularly in terms of real wages and the harm inflicted on public services), property owners' living standards continued to rise at the expense of those of renters. Thus, for a long time over the course of the past forty years, landlords and home-owners saw their interests flourish alongside each other. The property owners of today – particularly those who bought at the relatively low costs of earlier decades – derive their financial security from price speculation, which in turn derives its value from a highly profitable rented sector.

But in 2008 the level of owner-occupation peaked, at just over 16 million households. Constant and dramatic price rises, coupled with stagnant wages, locked ever more people out of ownership in the wake of the financial crisis. Instead, what had started as a by-product of Thatcherism (the growth of multiple-property-owners) has become a more prominent feature. What this means is that the state's project of shoring up house prices has been helping an ever-smaller number of owner-occupiers; and meanwhile, as the number of private renters have continued to rise, the government and the renting public have been increasingly propping up a very large landlord class. The idea of 'asset-based welfare' makes diminishing sense in a context where it is this large and growing number of landlords, rather than homeowners, who are increasingly its beneficiaries.

The irony, of course, is that the generation that did benefit from the rentier-driven boom in housing wealth did not in fact need the financial support that 'asset-based welfare' was intended to provide. Baby boomers benefited from a rise in living standards over the course of their working-age lives that succeeding generations found to be not just absent, but driven into reverse. A 2022 report from the Resolution Foundation pointed out that wages typically increased by 33 per cent every decade between 1970 and 2007 – but since 2007 they have not grown at all. This means that '8 million younger Brits have never worked in an economy that has sustained rising average wages'.[25]

These younger generations have also seen the dismantling of pensions, the increasing privatisation of the NHS, the failure of the social care system, and the hollowing out of public services under austerity and inflation shocks – and, as they grew older, homes had become so valuable that 'generation rent' was priced out of buying its own personal welfare system. Even the younger people who are able to buy homes will not enjoy nearly the same benefits: older owner-occupiers, who bought cheap and have paid off their mortgages, will be much better off than younger buyers facing rising interest rates and falling property prices. The implementation of asset-based welfare was initiated at the wrong time to achieve its stated aims: one generation won twice, while another lost twice.

Rehabilitating Rigsby

Given the huge number of landlords, and given that my work concerns housing, it is perhaps unsurprising that I meet landlords from time to time, and that the conversation sometimes drifts towards their own consciences. They seem to need reassurance – although the request is often delivered in very strident and defensive terms – that they are doing the right thing. They have worked very hard to buy property; they are an 'accidental' landlord; their tenant is very happy; or someone else would be charging much more. But what they come to discover is that virtually every landlord who is not making a loss is not just profiting at the tenant's expense, but doing so three times over. First, there is the rental profit, of course (anything that exceeds the costs of servicing the mortgage and upkeep). Second, the tenant is paying off the landlord's debt by gradually buying the landlord's asset for them. And, third, under the conditions that have prevailed over the last forty years, the property is gaining an astonishing amount of value. In fact, capital gains are so fruitful that the very act of ownership generates more wealth than the average income: the average house price increased by £31,000

per annum in 2020–21, while median household income stood at
£29,000.[26]

All of this involves almost no effort at all, and indeed many
landlords abdicate any form of labour altogether by hiring lettings
agents at the cost of a portion of their profits. Landlords may think
they work hard – but not nearly as hard as the average tenant has
to in order to pay the rent. Some even make the mistake of thinking
that landlords *provide* homes, rather than buying the homes that
already exist and leasing them out for profit.

But, as Brett Christophers reminds us in *Rentier Capitalism*, it is
easy to fall into the trap of moralising about landlords' 'unearned'
income, arguing that it somehow undermines the dignity of productive labour. Capital exploits our need for wages; landlords
exploit our need for shelter. It is odd to be more incensed by one
than the other. It is, of course, important to have answers to questions such as: Are 'accidental' landlords qualitatively different
from 'normal' landlords? (No), and: Shouldn't we be focusing on
'rogue' landlords, because most landlords are good? (Also no). But
the more important task when we are discussing the housing crisis
is to explore how today's landlords came to take their place in
society. How did we come to lose sight of the critique of landlordism (which is, necessarily, often couched in moral terms)? The
reason landlords feel the need to ask those conscience-salving
questions in the first place is because landlordism and passive
income from house-owning have come to be seen as benign,
although – deep down – landlords must know they are not.

In 1990 the Pogues released a single called 'Summer in Siam', the
B-side of which was their version of a traditional folk song called
'Bastard Landlord'. Shane McGowan's slightly off-tempo drawl
tells a story that is unthinkable to us today. The narrator had moved
from the countryside to London during the Second World War, to
a 'house by the river where the rent it was cheap'. Because all tenancies up until the 1990s would have been secure and rent-controlled,

McGowan's narrator (perfectly realistically) remains in his Thames-side rental for the next forty-four years ('My children were born here, it's here I'll grow old'). But the track is driven by its bitterness towards the eponymous villain. Despite how much of a bargain the tenant's situation seems to the modern listener, the lyrics curse the greed and indolence of the landlord, as the narrator watches his assets rise in value, each chorus ending: 'They'll carve your name where you lie / and I for one no tears will cry'.

Of course, it is unwise to try to glean social attitudes towards landlords from the B-side of a single that peaked at number sixty-four. But there is real evidence that landlords throughout the twentieth century were held in well-deserved contempt. Research from Heriot-Watt University indicates that the legacy of the war-time profiteers, the Rachman scandal, cultural figures like the miserly Rigsby from the sitcom *Rising Damp*, and public experience in general had led to a conception of the landlord as a politically toxic figure.

Even in 2001, the head of the Residential Landlords Association complained: 'We are always referred to as "bad", "rogue" or "slum" landlords. Commentators, in moments of generosity, often acknowledge that there are "some good landlords", implying that they are as rare as slates on a thatched roof.'[27] By the end of the twentieth century rented housing had become so unprofitable that the private sector had retreated to the most miserable types of housing, let by the most despicable types of profiteer. The only landlords left were those schemers who had cheated the death of the private rented sector. High-profile landlords at the time included the archly villainous Nicholas van Hoogstraaten – a millionaire, a racist thug and a major landowner on the south coast – whose crimes included paying a gang to throw a grenade through a rabbi's window. The simple fact is that, if the private rented sector was going to be revived, it needed a whole new class of landlord with a more palatable public image.

Following the deregulation of private tenancies in the 1980s, social attitudes softened. With such a large section of society taking part, playing the property market could not possibly be the avaricious and base activity of the popular imagination. The buy-to-let boom saw the invention of 'dinner party landlords': respectable middle-class people who were exploiting people's housing need as a sideline rather than their main job, and could talk about their hobby without disgrace. Their handsome profits were, after all, gained with the blessing of the law.

Popular culture also played its part. In the 1990s and early 2000s, the daytime TV schedules – and even some prime-time slots – were filled with endless property programmes, which no doubt still constitute a mainstay of social consciousness. A *Guardian* article from 2003 lists no fewer than eleven of 'the big players in TV's property market' that were airing at the time.[28] These played broadly the same role as TV gameshows: the audience rooted, in a low-key sort of way, for the 2-D characters who were hoping to win big by buying in the right place for the right price. Playing the property market, like going on *Deal or No Deal*, was as benign as it was banal.

What is striking about this laundering of property speculation in the years before the housing crisis really started to bite – what shows us that it had worked – is the change in our approach to the 'rogue landlord'. In 2001 the RLA had been complaining that 'rogue' was the default setting, and that good landlords were viewed as being exceptionally rare. Today the government talks about a 'small minority' of rogue landlords, estimated at just 10,500 (a tiny fraction of the 2.5 million total).[29] Even a Jeremy Corbyn–led Labour Party claimed that 'many landlords provide decent homes that tenants are happy with, but the Conservatives have gifted rogue landlords the freedom to flourish'.[30] The accepted wisdom twenty years after the buy-to-let boom, and despite the very serious decline in renters' rights that has gone with it, seems to be that *good* landlords are the norm, and *rogue* landlords are the slates on the thatched roof.

In the wake of the Rachman scandal, many (including the conservative *Sunday Times*) were horrified that property professionals such as lawyers and accountants were willing to 'pervert their professional ability' by using company arrangements to minimise their tax liabilities and maximise their operating flexibility.[31] Today, society is no longer scandalised: we have seen both a massive increase in the scale of the professional operation, with giant estate agents and letting websites, and the transformation of landlordism into a respectable activity for ordinary members of society.

The dominant ideology around landlordism has changed dramatically, and in some cases we can see the physical remains of that metamorphosis. On the Cressingham Gardens Estate, an award-winning 1970s council development – now slated for an all-too-familiar 'redevelopment' by Lambeth Council – there are two blue plaques side-by-side. One commemorates the council's chief architect, a communist called Ted Hollamby. The other commemorates John Major, who was then one of the Tory councillors responsible for getting the estate built, before going on to oversee the genesis of the buy-to-let boom as prime minister. Thus was the 1970s consensus in favour of council housing, as private landlords looked set to go the way of the dinosaurs, transformed into a consensus in the other direction. By 2006, even the homelessness charity Shelter was parroting the incomprehensible line that private landlords 'play a crucial role in providing homes'.[32] Over the course of thirty-five years, Thatcher's landlords won our hearts and minds.

Better the Landlord You Know

This phenomenon of a multiple-property-owning democracy – the state-sponsored expansion of the petty landlord class – has several interesting consequences that help to explain the nature of the housing crisis in Britain.

First, the idea of landlord in Britain is unlikely to summon an image of a faceless organisation or distant ghoul. Given the one-in-twenty-six-people statistic, the fact is that almost all of us know someone who is a landlord, or who is closely related to one. While being a landlord has obvious and inherent consequences in terms of wealth and social class, they are not the 1 per cent of the 1 per cent they are sometimes portrayed as being; strikingly, the 2021 English National Landlord Survey found that landlords' median income, excluding rents, was a relatively modest £24,000.

Nor is Britain's situation similar to, say, that of Madrid, Barcelona or Berlin, where there is increasing concern about housing estates in local neighbourhoods being directly controlled by high finance. Instead, landlords are deeply integrated into everyday society. This social intimacy affects societal attitudes towards landlords as a class. It tempers the sense of class conflict and disguises the extractive and exploitative nature of landlordism. It is difficult to imagine a serious project of decommodification, let alone more ambitious ideas like the expropriation of buy-to-lets for social housing, when so many people's perception of the average landlord is that they are just someone's aunt. 'Do you know . . . what the trees say when the axe comes into the forest?' asked John Berger in his novel *Once in Europa*. 'When the axe comes into the forest, the trees say: "Look! The handle is one of us!"'

Even if the idea of asset-based welfare does not apply to us directly, a huge proportion of the population is only one or two steps removed from someone who would face disaster if the rental market collapsed. The fates of landlords and homeowners are intertwined, which means that anyone who does not want to see homeowners suffer must support a lucrative private rented sector. To that extent, and on the basis that we care about the material welfare of the people in our lives, we are all encouraged to be at least a little bit invested in the project of asset-based welfare. The benefits of landed property, once so strictly concentrated within the aristocratic class, have been gradually dispersed over many centuries. But the sophistication of Thatcherism is that we are now *all* encouraged to act as a bulwark defending property rights, because we are all incentivised to fear the consequences of a failing housing market, whether on behalf of ourselves or others we know.

Social acceptance of landlordism is by no means universal. There are, of course, many people who understand all too well the misery that landlords cause. And an anti-landlord consciousness seems to be swelling, which is no doubt due to the impressive renters' movement that has grown stronger and more confident in recent years, and the associated personal experiences of a whole generation of renters. The point here is not to indulge friendly attitudes to landlordism, but to recognise that sympathy for the landlord does in fact exist in society after so many decades of consent-manufacturing.

The task of the housing movement is to raise political consciousness with this fact in mind: our job has been made harder by social conditions and decades of powerful apologetics for landlords. Chauvinist, often explicitly murderous anti-landlord rhetoric may well upset precisely the people we need to convince, and – if we are serious about building a large and cohesive movement – the question of how we persuade people of the need to abolish landlordism is a matter of debate.

The issue of landlords being normalised as our peers reared its head during the early stages of the pandemic, when the Labour Party dismissed calls for rent suspensions, partly out of concern for

landlords' human rights. This argument – while being simultaneously legally well-founded and ethically bizarre – does have at
least some force, when 93 per cent of people's landlords are human
beings, rather than corporations. Their humanity does, after all,
endow them with certain inalienable rights, including the right
to respect for property, which is foundational to all capitalist
societies.

Since then, the question of landlords' human rights has continued to spring up whenever the devolved administrations have tried
to implement housing reform. As long as the overwhelming majority of landlords have a brain rather than a boardroom, this issue of
landlords' rights is going to carry some weight among the public,
policymakers and the courts. Calls to solve the housing crisis
through the decommodification of people's property are bound to
be met with some institutional and popular caution.

Second, as well as affecting social perceptions of landlords as a
class, the social fact that landlords are people we know, rather than
faceless corporations, can sometimes humanise our own landlords,
erasing the inherent conflict and exploitation that the landlord–
tenant relationship creates. A friend recently asked me for help
with a renting problem (as you might expect, this happens to me
quite a lot), as her lettings agent was being difficult over a perpetually leaking pipe. After many weeks, one Friday evening, the leak
suddenly got much worse. When my friend reported it the agent
rang her, with a sudden uncharacteristic and obsequious burst of
good manners and friendliness, explaining that an emergency
plumber at a weekend would cost between £400 and £500. Could
my friend do without water over the weekend, the agent asked, as
he just could not possibly bear to ask the landlord to spend that
much.

This, of course, is irrespective of the fact that plumbers' fees, as
a legitimate business expense, would presumably be tax deductible
for the landlord. It's irrespective of the fact that it was the

landlord's own choice if they didn't have insurance. And it's irrespective of the fact that the agent could – and indeed did – bear to ask my friend to spend much more than £500 in excess water bills over the course of the leak. But the agent was banking on the fact that many renters would immediately relate to an actual person who was facing a sudden large spending commitment, and that their basic sense of empathy might persuade them to go a few days without water to avoid that situation.

Anyone who has ever worked in the third sector, or for a very small organisation, may recognise this dissolution or disguising of inherent conflicts. Calls for unionisation or pay rises in noncorporate environments are often met with appeals to the worker's heart. The worker is asked to empathise with the personal difficulties of the manager, who is their friend and also a nice person. The business is too small, too impecunious, to give its staff better working conditions or pay, although *of course* they would like to do so. We are encouraged to approach them with an almost apologetic attitude – to avoid creating an imposition, to pull together for the common good.

This seems to be a feature of the private rented sector, too. Many tenants I speak to are extremely forgiving towards their dreadful landlords. Many have come to see their own landlords as small business people with their own difficulties: a personal acquaintance – if not quite a friend – towards whom they wish no particular harm. Of course, this has a lot to do with the fear of eviction; but no doubt the fact that so many of our landlords are living and breathing people, of apparently ordinary means, also does a great deal to determine people's attitudes and behaviour towards them.

This phenomenon of humanisation – unlike my friend's water – runs hot and cold. In court, landlords will often try to appeal to a sense of humanity – whether mine, my client's or the judge's – by painting themselves as struggling small entrepreneurs with a regrettable and expensive problem on their hands: poor fellows who are simply in over their head. But an even more common approach is to meet my objection to their making someone homeless by claiming that they 'just want their property back'. It is a business decision – nothing personal – and the landlord is merely exercising a right that has been written into law.

This inhumane attitude does not spring from nowhere. The distinctive aspect of 'no-fault' evictions under section 21 is that they rely on an explicit promise by the state that – as long as certain procedural requirements are met – the landlord has an absolute right to an eviction. 'I just want my property back', which contains a suggestion that the decision is somehow ethically neutral because it reflects a legal entitlement, is a lament that has been created over the last few decades by a deep-seated legislative reality. Section 21 was not a legal measure that simply reflected a pre-existing social attitude.

In 2016 the UK Supreme Court was tasked with deciding whether this 'no-fault' eviction regime adequately protected renters' basic human rights.[33] Its judgment was interesting, because the court had to examine the policy background behind the system of insecure private tenancies and explain their purpose. Their comments are the closest thing to a historical-materialist analysis that I have ever seen in a judicial precedent. The court noted the Thatcher government's intention – undisturbed by later governments of any stripe – that 'the letting of private property will again become an economic proposition', and to make 'renting out property a much more attractive alternative for owners'. In other words, tenants' rights had been pared back deliberately to attract capital investment, and New Labour and later Conservative governments carried that same ideology forward.

The tenant lost the case, as the court decided that parliament's erosion of renters' rights since the 1980s reflected 'the state's assessment of where to strike the balance between the rights of residential tenants and the rights of private sector landlords'. Parliament had decided that 'I just want my property back' is a perfectly legitimate standpoint, bearing in mind landlords' human rights, and the court would not interfere with the MPs' decision in that respect.

This ruling was in striking contrast with the attitude towards evictions that the courts had displayed before the first Thatcher government. In a 1977 illegal eviction case, Lord Justice Lawton said that the landlord concerned 'at times seemed to be suggesting that this was a comparatively minor dispute between a landlord and a tenant. I emphatically disassociate myself from that. To deprive a man [*sic*] of a roof over his head in my judgment is one of the worst torts which can be committed. It causes stress, worry and anxiety.'[34] Lawton was no bleeding-heart judicial activist – at the beginning of his career he was openly a member of the British Union of Fascists – but it is probably fair to say that his attitude towards evictions reflected the legal and social reality of the day, before tenants' rights were so comprehensively dismantled.

The attitude that landlords are just everyday people is thus a one-way process; in contrast, tenants have become dehumanised. Law and society have lost sight of the fact that depriving someone of the roof over their head has the most serious consequences for their lives. Even in the most compelling cases, if the landlord has a valid 'no-fault' eviction claim, there tends to be no legal defence against it, and the court has no choice but to evict. After all, this bizarre system was put in place with the quite candid intention that renting out homes would become a more profitable business. As Victor Hugo memorably put it, 'There are fearsome moments in our civilization; those when the law decrees a shipwreck, a total ruin.'[35] That line has often come to mind on the frequent occasions when I have had to advise someone that there is simply no defence against an eviction claim: that the court must and will order them to leave their home.

Third, the nature of the conflict between homeowners' and renters' interests is unusual in Britain, and underlies a serious social unease. The housing question is not class conflict in the usual sense – between the ranks of working people on one hand and capital on the other – but rather a state of civil war. Younger people are pitted against their own parents. Workers who rent, and thus need housing costs to stay as low as possible, are completely at odds with their homeowner colleagues, who delight in the rising value of their asset.

Likewise, a homeowner on a particular street might be thrilled to see or take part in the gentrifying processes that go hand-in-hand with rising house prices, or by the benefits – pleasant cafés, better transport links, and so on – that are so often associated with social cleansing. Meanwhile, a tenant next door may shudder at the prospect of being driven out by rent increases.

When Marx wrote about landowners as one of the 'three great classes in society' – the others being the bourgeoisie, who own the means of production, and the working class – he had in mind the great institutional rentiers of earlier centuries: the Church, the Crown, landed estates. While, in some parts of the modern world, this landowning class has come to be replaced by a somewhat coherent group of rentier institutions (corporate landlords, mortgage lenders and institutional investors), landlordism in Britain is distributed among 2.5 million fairly ordinary people. These landlords' interests are aligned with those of the nearly 15 million owner-occupiers whose prosperity relies on property, and therefore on a strong rental market.

This deep embedding of rentiers within society means that we have to pursue two contradictory economic and social aims at the same time. The state cannot fail the homeowning class, given that it has deliberately fostered a culture of dependency on passive income to replace pensions, wages and social services. At the same time, the state absolutely *must* fail them if it intends to do anything meaningful about the crisis of housing affordability.

We have reached a particularly fragile state of affairs in which this battle over housing costs is being fought at such close quarters that the nuclear family unit is now divided internally. Where homeowners have grown-up children who rent, there is an obvious internal division between the policies that would serve those two generations. But each side – the parents and the children – are themselves conflicted internally, too. From the parents' perspective, their own wealth – and their children's inheritance – must be maintained; but equally they must surely loathe a system that causes their children to spend such a great deal of money on poor-quality rented housing, and locked out of homeownership.

From the children's perspective this experience is reversed: they have a clear interest in ending the system of price rises that keeps them trapped in the renting system, but they would presumably dread to see their parents' financial security for later life come to harm. The creation of a large petty-bourgeois rentier class – a whole generation dependent on housing wealth – means that the civil war over housing policy is fought between parents and children, between neighbours and colleagues, and, as Chapter 4 will explore, between regions of the country.

Fourth, the large rentier class that now exists is an important electoral constituency. The one unifying interest of the fairly disparate voter coalition that led to the Conservatives' electoral successes since 2010 is homeownership, served by the 'implicit promise', as Adam Blanden puts it, 'to protect housing wealth'.[36] This sets Britain apart from many other countries. In Germany, for example, one of the more powerful demands made on the government by businesses is to keep housing costs under control in order to keep the wage bill down.[37] In Hong Kong – one of the most densely populated places in the world – the challenge for policy-makers has been how to maintain the territory's soaring land values while preventing correspondingly high rents from obliterating its supply of cheap labour.[38] In California, housing costs are now so high that Silicon Valley companies are increasingly troubled by the sensational wages that they must offer their staff, while San

Francisco itself begins to lose its lustre for tech workers because low-paid service workers – restaurant and shop staff, minicab drivers, cleaners – are priced out of the city, and quality of life for the rich declines as a result.[39]

Of the three 'great classes', two – capital and labour – traditionally make the same demand for lower rents. In contemporary Britain, however, a powerful electoral bloc is demanding a steady and constant *increase* in housing costs: the most powerful pressures on housing policy come from an electoral base of petty-bourgeois Tories, rather than from big capital. Given the electoral plurality of homeowners weaned on housing wealth, there is going to be very significant pressure on the state to ensure that prices continue to rise.

In *Capital and Land*, published in 1978, Doreen Massey and Alejandrina Catalano argued that Marx's understanding of landowners as a homogeneous group with a shared interest no longer held true: they pointed out that the class of rentiers had become rather motley and heterogeneous compared to previous centuries. It is fair to acknowledge that the class of landlords and speculating homeowners has only grown larger and more disparate since then; but it is also important to note that landowners in fact remain unified in their desire to see rents and land prices climb. One of Marx's 'three great classes' has simply become a larger group of individuals, thereby intensifying the social and economic conflict over the cost of accommodation.

In response, British employers seem to have taken a more relaxed view of rising land costs than their peers in Germany and elsewhere. The calculation of British capital appears to be that its homeowning employees can count on house-price growth to compensate them for wage stagnation, while tenant workers are forced to put in more hours for their employers just to ensure that they can continue to meet the rent.

Generation Rentier

Why do landlords put the rent up? It may seem like an odd question – even a naive one – but it is worth considering. Given the individualised nature of landlordism in Britain, rent increases are often castigated as a personal choice, or even a moral one, on the part of the landlord. But, even assuming that a landlord's costs remain stable (which is not a foregone conclusion, given the massive impact that interest rates will have on interest-only buy-to-let mortgages), there are more structural pressures at work that are worth understanding.

Marx would argue that there is an economic impetus to raise rents. Housing – like all financial investments – has to generate a yield that corresponds to its speculative value. Landlords need to be able to show that the purchase price of housing is justified, and the idea of ever-increasing rents is baked into that purchase price. Landlords will have bought homes – or will intend to sell them – at a price that assumes ever-rising rents, and the actual rent charged will need to correspond to the value of the property. Just as land in general requires the existence of rent to justify its value, a buoyant property market like ours requires rents to rise perpetually.

In other words, by failing to charge the highest possible rent at all times, landlords run the risk of signalling or even contributing to the devaluation of their own asset. Rent increases are thus a broad economic phenomenon, and cannot be put down to the peccadillos or exceptional selfishness of 2.5 million individual people. Instead, every day the class of landlords asks the class of tenants to confirm and maintain the value of homeowners' investments, and every day tenants answer the call.

This has an impact on housing conditions, too. In the example given in Chapter 1, the buyer of a house with an annual rent of £12,000 (and an expectation of rising rents) ought to factor in the cost of upkeep, repairs and improvement: boilers break down, damp-proof courses need replacing, sash windows are notoriously leaky. Those are significant costs. If a culture existed in which landlords looked after their tenants' homes conscientiously, they would have to calculate their assets as being much less valuable: the calculation ought to be £240,000, *plus* anticipated rent rises, *minus* anticipated costs of repairs. But instead, landlords tend to treat their anticipated rental income as an absolute right. The silent compulsion of precarious tenancies, disciplining the class of renters, means that requests for landlords to honour their legal obligations to keep homes in good repair are treated as extraordinary and outrageous – and this attitude is factored into the anticipated yield. Disrepair thus benefits landlords as a class, because this social acceptance of the fact that no works will be carried out contributes to reliable rental yields and rising house prices. Sadly, this is nothing new, as the following evidence to an 1840 parliamentary committee shows:

Q. Do the landlords exact high rents from them?

A. Extremely high.

Q. Do the landlords appear to give much attention to the decent condition of the dwellings from which they derive so large a rent?

A. Just the reverse.[40]

Given the experience of rack-renting after the partial liberalisation of the private sector in the 1950s, it would have been obvious to anyone that this sort of extortion is exactly what the wholesale deregulation of the 1980s and 1990s would achieve. Writing while the 1988 Housing Act was still making its way through parliament, social scientist Perri 6 (now a professor at Queen Mary University of London) predicted: 'The results will be exorbitant rents, massive profits for finance houses and developers and homelessness on a scale to dwarf even today's figures.' He went on:

Tenants will be forcibly moved around to create new lettings, pushed into rent arrears by high rents, made homeless and the houses sold for owner occupation. Winkling and harassment for vacant possession will be rife as after the last decontrol in 1957 . . . Councils will soon have insufficient housing for the homeless . . . The years of preparation for this counter revolution in housing have given us a foretaste of the free market. The full reality may be unimaginable now but in a very few years we may be working with it daily, and our clients experiencing the full misery of its freedom.[41]

This prediction foresaw the harm of deregulation, but did not get the method quite right. Perri 6 did not anticipate that, as the erosion of tenants' rights bedded into social consciousness, landlords would find no need to resort to 'winkling and harassment'. As we saw in the case of Ana given in Chapter 1, and as the experience of so many renters tells us, the current practice is for landlords simply to ask us to leave and/or to tell us that the rent is going up. But this took time to unfold, of course. It was two years *after* the 1988 Act was passed that Shane McGowan was grumbling about renting the same house for forty-four years.

It was only as the financialisation of homes became more generalised over the next few decades that we developed a common understanding – a structure of feeling – around the fact that landlords can always raise the rent or evict us because they have us in check. Gradually, we came to a point where we saw, as David Harvey puts it, the 'treatment of land as a pure financial asset, and the reduction of landholders to a faction of money capitalists who have simply chosen, for whatever reason, to hold a claim on rent'.[42]

It was as this process unfolded that a behavioural and ideological change took place. One of the more important things that I do is to provide 'know your rights' training to community groups and trade unions. The thing that I have to impress upon attendees, which is often a revelation, is that private tenants do not have to leave when the landlord asks them to. They do not even have to leave when a section 21 notice expires, because – as a matter of law – their right to occupy does not come to an end until the landlord lawfully evicts them by obtaining a court order, and then a bailiff's warrant.

The awesome power of the 'no-fault' eviction regime is derived from the incredibly strong social awareness of landlords' absolute dominion over us, which is an understanding that has developed over time. This has made us remarkably meek when it comes to insisting on what little legal entitlement we do have. In other words, just as 'generation rentier' came to understand just how strong their bargaining position was under the regime inaugurated by the 1988 Act, tenants reached the same conclusion.

It was by this method that residential rent extraction came to take its place in British society. A net gain of 2 million landlords over the course of my lifetime – a whole little class with a trade that was somehow cloaked in a new-found respectability – has built a property market that has become a mainstay of the national economy. Landlordism has become such a widespread phenomenon that homelessness charities can now profit from the rental market without blushing.

And generation rentier is, of course, funded by generation rent. It is younger and poorer people who maintain the value of homeowners' assets by paying the rent. While many have written about the massive transfer of wealth that will one day occur when the current generation of homeowners dies, passing on their property through inheritance, perhaps the more important point is this longstanding transfer of wealth from younger renters to the older generation. It is tenants who have been underwriting housing values, and thereby paying for the pensions and later-life welfare of generation rentier. The question, as renters' living standards continue to fall, is whether and for how long this situation is sustainable. The trouble with Thatcherism, it turns out, is that you eventually run out of other people's money.

4

Solving Things Ourselves:
Tenant Organising

It's not sufficient to rely on the law to help us. The law is very elastic, and the government sees to it that it stretches the landlords' way.

Tenants in Revolt (1939 film)

In 2015, the London Borough of Southwark settled a high-profile legal challenge brought by a homeless Iranian refugee against the council's homelessness 'gatekeeping' practices.[1] Gatekeeping is a system of procedures – formal or informal – designed to dissuade people from presenting themselves to councils' housing departments, thus avoiding the expensive and complex legal obligations that tend to arise the moment a homeless person walks through a local authority's door. By definition, gatekeeping is almost impossible to challenge in the courts: nothing happens on the record, so evidence is often lacking. But Southwark's internal documents and public leaflets were so remarkably frank about their unlawful tactics that the council threw in the towel and agreed to be bound by a court order restraining it from acting illegally.

The gatekeeping did not stop, though. Over and over again, people who sought help from Southwark's housing office were turned away, given the wrong information, or told to sort their situations out themselves. Many of them eventually approached Housing Action Southwark and Lambeth (HASL), which noticed that the systemic gatekeeping was still going on, despite the obligations under the High Court's order.

HASL decided to try to tackle the problem at its source by going along to the housing office to try to catch Southwark in the act, and stopping the gatekeeping from happening. In a series of actions that were part protest and part practical assistance, HASL members turned up with leaflets, clipboards and banners. People who were sent away were encouraged to go back in, newly armed with 'know your rights' factsheets, and advised not to leave until something had been done. The council was furious. When remonstrative security guards failed to persuade HASL to leave, the council took to shutting down the housing office whenever HASL members were there. On one particularly miserable occasion, on a desperately hot day, a heavily pregnant applicant who had come to ask where the council planned to rehouse her once her baby was born was met with security-grilled doors, and told by security staff that it was HASL's fault that the office was shut.

Taking stock, HASL realised that the council could outmanoeuvre them if it just kept closing down the housing office each time they turned up. It was disgraceful and infantile behaviour, but it was working. But it could not, HASL thought, shut down a major local authority's housing department every day. So, members decided to turn up every day and see what happened. Over the course of a few weeks, by degrees, things started to improve. The security guards became inured to the flow of applicants, and were less visibly hostile towards them. The doors stopped slamming shut, and fewer people were sent away with a flea in their ear. In short, a few leafleteers with clipboards were succeeding where the law, in all its majesty, had failed.

Change – particularly in times of crisis and darkness – tends to come from below. We know with certainty that patrician charitable housing schemes can only help a small number of people, and that things only really improve when more systemic shifts take place. We also know, from the history of the twentieth century in particular, that genuine victories tend to spring from social movements and direct action, or at least activism working in tandem with radical governance. And housing lends itself well to political activity, both at the street and legislative levels.

Housing problems confront us immediately, and every day. The injustices of the system, which routinely entail poorer people transferring the bulk of their wages to richer people for a poor-quality 'service', are staggering. While workplaces are often successful at disguising or mediating the exploitative nature of waged labour, the housing system is so obviously unfair that many people seem to come to it as something of a gateway to political activism. A government inquiry as far back as 1917 found that poor housing conditions were a major element in causing industrial unrest.[2] The horrors of the present day have seen an upswing of the housing movement in Britain in recent years.

But what does it take to change things? How do we move from a model of collective housing support in a time of emergency to a position of achieving broader goals? Despite the gathering strength of the housing movement, and the glaring need for things to stop getting worse, the movement in Britain feels less emboldened than, say, its counterpart in Berlin, where campaigners have forced stronger rent controls onto the agenda, or Barcelona, where well-organised groups coalesce around neighbourhoods.

As discussed in Chapter 3, the 'no-fault' evictions regime has caused many renters' sense of resistance to evaporate gradually since the 1980s: landlords' power has become hegemonic, and it will take some time to recover our strength and courage – though things are beginning to turn. At critical moments like this, it is worth asking how housing movements succeed, and reflecting on whether we are doing things in the right way: 'Thinking in order to do,' as A. Sivanandan put it, 'not thinking in order to think.'[3]

Revolt on the Clyde

The rent controls that formed a cornerstone of housing policy in the long period between the First World War and the Thatcher-to-Blair era did not spring from nowhere. Nor were they handed down by an enlightened government, conscious of the economic benefits of lower living costs. They were prised, instead, from the hands of a terrified wartime administration.

In the years leading up to the First World War, a mixture of wage restraint and resistance to pro-war jingoism had energised a fiery trade union movement in Scotland's Clyde Valley, where factory production and shipyards were critical to the war effort. At the same time, landlords were profiteering from the wartime conditions by raising rents. In response, a women-led campaign, with Govan resident Mary Barbour as its figurehead, organised a devastating movement of rent strikes and eviction resistance. The campaign's simple slogan was 'We are not paying increased rent', and they meant it.

Although the landlords went to court to try to evict the defaulting households, community resistance to court orders was fierce and effective. The sheriff's officers (known as bailiffs in England and Wales) were routinely defeated and humiliated by rapidly mobilised residents when they tried to turn people out. Faced with a powerful social movement, the law was failing to gain any traction in the real world, and court orders were reduced to a legal fiction.

Like so many periods of successful social mobilisation, the 'Red Clydeside' era came to be distinguished by its effective solidarity and its action on a number of different fronts. The eviction resisters and trade unionists melded their struggles together. Interestingly, though, this was a result of the behaviour of their opponents, rather than a strategic decision of their own. Frustrated by Barbour's fearsome tactics, and unable to turn the striking tenants onto the streets, the landlords came up with the legal innovation of applying to the court to attach rental debts to household wages: they would enforce their claims not through evictions, but by garnishing tenants' wage packets in an effort to break their resolve. This initially met with success, as despondent workers came home one-by-one with half of their wages missing. But the hapless landlords then made the mistake of creating a flashpoint: they issued summonses to a whole group of tenants employed in Glasgow's shipyards. The case came to court in November 1915.

The landlords had dislodged a boulder. 'On the day of the trial', as trade unionist and later Communist Party MP Willie Gallacher recalled,

> Glasgow witnessed a demonstration the like of which had never been seen before. From early morning the women were marching to the centre of the city where the sheriff's court is situated. Mrs Barbour's army was on the march. But even as they marched, mighty reinforcements were coming from the workshops and the yards. From far away Dulmuir in the West, from Parkhead in the East, from Cathcart in the South and Hydepark in the North, the dungareed army of the proletariat invaded the centre of the city.[4]

The unions threatened to strike if the court went ahead with docking the wages. But, worse than that, the militancy that had been brewing in the union, housing and anti-war movements promised to erupt. 'The roars from outside the court', Gallacher wrote, 'were making the windows rattle. At any point the deputation [of tenants] might be followed by a surging, irresistible crowd of angry men and women.'[5] Glasgow was on the point of enormous civil unrest. The solicitor representing the claimant in the trial – a landlord's agent – put a call through to David Lloyd George, the minister of munitions, who urged him to drop the case pending government action.

He followed this advice, which caused 'a scene of enthusiasm that baffles description. Shouting, singing, cheering . . . All night long the celebration of victory went on.'[6] The Scotland minister, Thomas McInnon Wood, recommended to Asquith's cabinet that rents be frozen, and within a month the progenitor of the Rent and Mortgage Interest Restriction Act 1915 (the 'Rent Acts') was in force, and rent controls remained in place more or less until the end of the century. Some Rent Act tenancies still exist today, and the protected tenants of the twentieth and early twenty-first centuries owe their rights in no small part to the militant Glaswegians of a century ago.

My friend and colleague David Watkinson, who has had a remarkable career representing squatters and homeless people since the 1970s, remarks that he was once explaining the origins of the Rent Acts to answer a legal question in court, and read out Willie Gallacher's account of the day of the Glasgow demonstration. The landlord's barrister responded – surely correctly – that 'this was the first time that the memoir of a communist MP had been read in support of a legal submission, and he was not saying that as a compliment'.[7]

The November 1915 moment of civil unrest succeeded in a very particular context. Clydeside's anger threatened to spread across wartime Britain, with marches also taking place in places like Northampton, Birmingham, London and Birkenhead, where thousands of women marched behind a banner declaring: 'Father is fighting in Flanders. We are fighting the landlords here.'[8] A contemporaneous article from suffragette newspaper *Women's Dreadnaught* reported on the cut and thrust of landlord–tenant relations: a piece called 'Fight against Grasping Landlords' cited many examples from across the country of rent-increase notices and countervailing strikes and eviction resistances on various scales.[9] This working-class militancy 'threatened to spread from an opposition to landlord profiteering to an opposition to all profiteering, and most notably to that of the armaments manufacturers'; landlords, the government decided, would have to take one for the team.[10] 'If "unrest" is to be converted into contentment,' King George V openly declared in a personal speech in 1919, 'the provision of good houses may prove one of the most potent agents in that conversion.'[11]

But Glasgow in particular, as well as being crucial to the war effort, had extraordinarily high levels of mortgaged housing at the time: about 90 per cent of homes were borrowed against, and most of them were tenanted.[12] The unrest in Glasgow thus posed a threat not just to the landlords themselves, but to the security of finance capital, to the local building societies, and possibly to the whole regional economy. The problem had to be solved.

There is something of a golden thread of threatened revolution and reactive housing policy running back through history. Just as the Asquith government under George V was terrified of popular wartime Bolshevism, the middle-class housing reformers of the nineteenth century were 'nurtured on memories of the Parisian Commune'. Historian Gareth Stedman Jones credits this anxiety about the Commune as one of the factors underlying late Victorian housing law reform.[13] Elsewhere, the 'Red Vienna' social housing programme – probably the apogee of decent housing under modern capitalism – was founded in the inherently compromising and anti-revolutionary ideology of Austro-Marxism. In fact, we can trace this tendency as far back as the decline of the Roman Empire. When the Gracchi brothers, two Roman statesmen, championed a project of redistributing privately owned farmland to the poor, 'The men of wealth and power . . . worked to turn the people against Tiberius [Gracchus], accusing him of trying to redistribute the land so as to take the lead in disrupting the political order, and setting in motion a revolution.'[14] The brothers were assassinated for their troubles, but their socialistic land project had become so popular that the Senate did not dare to reverse it.

Clydeside's mantle was taken up by other radical movements over the course of the next hundred years. Where they were successful, the common elements seem to be weakened or crisis-ridden governments, strong social movements, radical goals and diabolical housing conditions. Throughout the 1930s – particularly in the East End of London – housing campaigns among slum-like dwellings were a recruiting ground for communists and anti-fascists. Their activities were aided and abetted by municipal socialist administrations and charitable projects. In the aftermath of the Second World War, a mass squatting movement was a self-organised expedient while the 'homes fit for heroes' were being built.

Squatting likewise played a significant role in the 1970s and 1980s, when there were ongoing scandals of empty homes and dreadful conditions. Squatting in the 1970s was particularly important to groups that were disproportionately prone to homelessness, notably Brixton's gay and lesbian and black squatting scenes, and Tower Hamlets' Bengali squatting movement. The latter made explicit reference to the threat of 'bloody revolution' on Clydeside when they promised the local authorities 'a good fight'.[15]

At the same time, a major fourteen-month rent strike by council tenants in Kirby in 1973 may have led to the eventual repeal of national legislation that had raised council rents. And in the present day, every day, housing groups were clawing back money from recalcitrant deposit holders, helping people to secure the homes they need from local authorities, and pestering landlords to carry out repairs. They were mobbing lettings agents and resisting evictions, and otherwise pouring sand into the gearbox of the housing-wealth-generation machine.

Political organisation around housing, when it works, can be powerfully effective. Over the last hundred years or so, mass movements focused on housing have made real advances on behalf of the working class. Periodically, the financial institutions of the City have had to step in to oppose or reverse these gains:

to protect the government from itself by restraining hard-won state spending on decent housing. In 1921, for example, a financial crisis provided the context for unpicking the post–First World War 'homes fit for heroes' housebuilding subsidies.[16] This happened again in 1947, under 'pressure from the City, and from the United States, which dangled the carrot of Marshall aid, to cut [government] expenditure, and particularly to divert resources from social legislation to infrastructural investment'.[17] The low council rents of the mid twentieth century, maintained through working-class power, came under attack through the Housing Finance Act 1972.

What Do We Want? When Do We Want It?

In 2016, a century on from the Revolt on the Clyde, I was taking part in a 'Kill the Bill' rally, opposing what went on to become the Housing and Planning Act 2016. The proposed legislation looked set to reduce social housing stocks even further, and to deliberately intensify the problem of rising house prices in an attempt to 'cajole' the housebuilding industry. As we gathered at Lincoln's Inn Fields in central London, the flags and placards of campaign groups and political organisations were raised in a festive melee.

But there, among the usual suspects, were the prominent banners of the local Labour Party branches of Southwark and Lambeth councils. Both boroughs had been one-party states for years, and it was those very Labour councils that local housing activists had come to see as our political opponents. They were certainly our adversaries in the day-to-day skirmishes of the housing crisis. But more broadly, their projects of gentrification-led development and social housing sell-offs were virtually inseparable from the ideology of the new Bill. How could the housing movement find itself making common cause with Blairite local governments? What did this say about our horizons?

Engels's analysis of political activity in the housing sphere was hopelessly despondent. As well as complaining that public concern about housing was cynical because it only ever emerged when things began to affect the middle class, he took the view that nothing meaningful could be done unless not just landlordism was abolished, but cities as well. And you cannot, he argued, simply legislate your way out of the housing crisis: you need to overthrow capitalism itself. Neither the state, nor charities, nor individual homeownership would alleviate housing hardship, so what was the point in campaigning at all?

This defeatism is unusual. Not only were there serious and successful anti-landlord movements both before and after Engels, but the improvements that were made when housing was partially decommodified in the twentieth century to some extent proved him wrong. There is, in fact, a great deal to fight for, even for those who take the view that capitalism will not disappear within our lifetimes. Frankly, it is surprising that someone who had written so vividly about squalor in *The Condition of the Working Class in England* could adopt such a high-handed posture against doing anything about it.

Set against Engels, there is a rich tradition of land and housing radicalism. The history books groan with examples of effective anti-landlord struggle. The seventeenth-century 'Diggers' movement used a lovely and much-quoted phrase about all landlords having originally obtained their land 'either by Oppression, or Murther, or Theft', although we have to be slightly wary of false friends: 'landlords' then were a workplace concept. They confronted workers in the sphere of production – namely, farming – long before they came to dominate housing, and production and housing have very different characteristics.

But Ellen Meiksins Wood argues: 'These popular forces . . . left a tremendous legacy of radical ideas quite distinct from the "progressive" impulses of capitalism, a legacy that is still alive today in various democratic and anti-capitalist movements.'[18] Wood is surely right to highlight the anti-commodification movements of more recent decades. Henri Lefebvre, too, in his influential 1968 book *The Right to The City*, argued that city-dwellers are capable of standing against commodification and capitalism.[19] He suggests that Marxism is capable of co-opting cities and curbing the worst excesses of capitalism in the built environment. More recently, Mike Davis's 'Who Will Build the Ark?' seeds ideas of community-based, small-scale, ecologically minded urban progress through popular engagement.[20]

But it is precisely because 'housing improvement under capitalism' is a vexed question that it is important to be clear about our aims. Ultimately, we want our living situations to be less bad. And while we have to be wary of the long tradition of governments acquiescing to housing reforms in order to sap any revolutionary potential, this must not lead us to Engels's defeatism. Millions of people are subject to insecure, overpriced and dreadful housing; and even if we fail to solve the broader problems of poverty and hardship that inevitably occur under capitalism, we owe it to each other to make things better. Squalor and harmful insecurity are rife, and they need not be.

This is a critical moment for framing the debate about our ambitions. In recent years there has been a troubling coalescence between the property developers' aim of building more homes and the demands of government and mainstream housing campaigners. There is a strand of 'YIMBY-ism' ('yes in my backyard'), imported from the United States, which threatens to dominate the narrative. This standpoint castigates any struggle against profit-driven redevelopment as 'NIMBY-ism' ('not in my backyard'), in a cynical attempt to force us into a fruitless debate about housing supply rather than engaging with the deeper problems of housing wealth. Given that building houses is one of the most carbon-intensive of all human activities, an important aim of this book has been to

highlight the legal and economic causes of the crisis, and to ensure
that the housing movement does not become distracted by the red
herring of supply arguments.

Something odd that defines so many housing campaigns now –
magnificent work though they do – is their opposition to 'luxury
flats'. It is easy to understand why, of course. Under the deep-rooted
prevailing orthodoxy that fetishes supply, neighbourhoods tend to
be torn apart, only to be replaced with buildings that are too expensive for the previous residents, while government and developers
both chalk this up as a win. There is a principled objection to social
cleansing, and it is unsurprising that a great deal of housing activism
expresses itself as a demand for the right not to be displaced.

But in 1939, groups like the Stepney Tenants' Defence League
had more robust ambitions. *Tenants in Revolt*, a film they made at
the time, and a charming piece of newsreel agitprop, documents
the tenants crossing the city from their squalid, overcrowded tenements to picket the landlord's house in a leafy suburb, and then at
his Central London office. 'When conditions are bad and rents are
high', the *Star Wars*–style opening crawl informs us, 'the people
under the correct leadership revolt and by uniting achieve their
objective.' And their objective, surprisingly enough, was luxury
flats. The film notes the horrifying levels of poverty-related infant
mortality at the heart of a vastly wealthy empire, but even as their
babies were dying from malnutrition their demands were more
sensational than ours. In fact they were the direct opposite. There
can be no principled objection to modern, well-designed homes;
the issue has only ever been whether we are to be allowed to live
in them.[21]

This is where the housing movement needs to pitch itself,
demanding not just security and affordability, but a move towards
the decommodification of housing to ensure universal access and
good conditions. We can do better than demanding the right to be
allowed to stay in expensive, inadequate homes.

Tar and Feathers

In recent years, I have been asked time and again to advise on the legality of rent strikes. Why are rent strikes so difficult? Why can't we emulate the tenants of the 1910s and 1930s, when neighbourhoods sprang into action and defeated their landlords through pure economic struggle? 'In Tooting the 350 rent strikers have won the day, the landlords after a stiff fight, agreeing to withdraw the increase', reported *Women's Dreadnought* in October 1915, citing it as an example of many such victories.[22] In 1939, more than 40,000 of Birmingham's council tenants racked up arrears of £20,000 by declaring a protracted strike (worth about £1 million in 2023).[23] What is stopping us from setting up little neighbourhood strikes of our own, and making this our political weapon of choice?

In Chapter 3, I described the peculiarly atomised nature of the British landlord class, which forces us to shoot at too many targets. It is difficult to take collective action when we lack a collective opponent – and particularly when landlords are able to evict us at will. But perhaps the more important answer is that, as a result of British legal and political history, rent strikes are illegal.

So what, you might ask, and dismiss this as a timid point. After all, the groundbreaking municipal socialist councillors of Poplar went to prison over tax rates, as it was 'better to break the law than break the poor'. But rent strikes are not illegal in the sense of 'you probably shouldn't do this', like cycling without reflectors or sharing your streaming passwords. Nor are they illegal in a way that lends itself to effective political martyrdom. They are illegal in a way that is specifically designed to undermine our effective methods of organising. Britain's strike laws are a national peculiarity that emerged during the early days of trade unionism. While many other jurisdictions have a codified 'right to strike', or even lack the legal restrictions that might make striking illegal in the first place, strikes in Britain are very narrowly protected through the imposition of *immunities* against the clever legal tactics of employers.

To cut a long story short, capital and its lawyers realised that they could crush the nascent trade union movement by suing the unions for the lost profits that any strikes had cost them, and they ran a number of successful cases through the courts to establish that principle. Parliament eventually intervened to prevent capitalists from pursuing the unions for damages – but only in very limited circumstances. Needless to say, those protections do not extend to rent strikes, and we run the risk that landlords will try to sue housing organisers themselves, and/or renters' unions as organisations, for *all* of the missing rent, rather than suing each individual tenant for the amount that each of them owes. The damages from a big rent strike could instantly bankrupt a group, which would be a particular concern for dues-paying organisations. And the bigger the strike, the more expensive the damages. Anti-strike laws in Britain are contrived to smash our organising capacity, and rent strikes are an incredibly high-risk strategy as the law currently stands.

But surely, those anti-strike laws applied just as much in 1915 as they do today? That is partially true, although the courts do not seem to have established the illegality of rent strikes until 1939–40. More importantly, however, there was a particular kismet to the 1915 rent strike movement. Similar strikes failed when conditions were not exactly right, including one in Leeds just eighteen months earlier, and another in Clydeside itself, supported by some 20,000 people, in 1922.[24] Not only was there a strong sense of cohesion within the 1915 movement – the solidarity of trade unions being particularly important – but both capital and government were more interested in resolving the dispute than in supporting the landlords' cause. The 1915 strike exposed the inherent economic tensions between landlords, on the one hand, who wanted to keep rents high, and employers, government and tenants on the other, who generally preferred them to be low. But the mischief of the current political economy of housing is that it coalesces landlords' interests with those of homeowners by making ever-rising rents the cornerstone of housing wealth. Given that homeownership is such a major part of the economy, the 1915-style tensions do not exist in the same way, and today's rent strikers would have few friends in high places. These days it is easy to imagine a rent strike being met with the same puce-faced rage summoned against the deposers of statues of slavers, or the high-impact actions of climate activists, rather than the secretary of state volunteering to impose immediate rent-capping legislation to help our cause.

The absence of recent major rent strikes in Britain speaks not to the failure of a too-timid housing movement, but to an understandable restraint on the part of groups that are refusing to play politics with people's lives. In too many cases, evictions and defeats are the most likely outcomes. Things may change, of course, as benefits begin to outweigh risks, but until now the housing movement has seemed realistic in recognising that tenants are too precarious, and the risks to the movement too high, for effective strikes to take place.

But this means that tenants have had to turn to other tactics, including the specific targeting and public shaming of landlords. This happens both in the private rental market, local housing groups often campaigning against individual slumlords and lettings agents, and – increasingly – in the social housing sphere: ITV News, the secretary of state and high-profile housing campaigners such as Kwajo Tweneboa have taken to shaming housing associations publicly by documenting their tenants' living conditions. Short of a drastic improvement in conditions, landlords may have to get used to exposure and public shame.

Who can blame the housing movement for protesting against landlords directly, for all that they may complain about it? What else are we supposed to do? On the one hand, rent strikes are virtually impossible. On the other, neither major political party has adopted any housing policies worth voting for in my lifetime (at least, not until things started to improve in 2019). There tends to be no legal defence when a landlord tries to evict someone, even when the moral case against an eviction might be overwhelming.

What are tenants supposed to do but try to humiliate the people who profit so handsomely from the housing crisis? Landlords *should* feel ashamed. They should cringe and wring their hands at taking such an active role in perpetuating the miseries we see today, and the public should be bitterly critical of them for it. That was how we felt about their grubby little trade before their image was so successfully rehabilitated in the 1990s, and it is only right that they should be on the front rank in the battles that housing crisis inevitably produces. Law, economics and politics are all on their side; the suggestion that they should also be immune from criticism is laughable. We should take heart from the old footage in *Tenants in Revolt*, when the East Enders took their placards and chants to the landlord's home and office to embarrass him in front of his neighbours, colleagues and clients. 'How outrageous!', the narrator sneers sarcastically, 'what an affront to the respectability of the district!'

Here to Stay, Here to Fight

Engels's pessimism stemmed from the fact that he viewed housing through an exclusively economic lens. He saw it as a secondary site of exploitation, which was less important than the struggles that take place in the workplace. Because it was labour, he claimed, that produced surplus value, the set-pieces of class struggle must take place in the employment setting, and housing was fundamentally only concerned with the act of buying. By that logic, he argued that housing movements were theoretically akin to a consumer rights group, rather than a labour union or political organisation proper.

But just forty years after *The Housing Question* was published, 20,000 women and men in Glasgow demanded and won rent controls, which went on to have fundamental consequences for the political economy of land: within sixty years of the revolt on the Clyde, landlordism was brought to its knees. Thereafter, it was then the deliberate re-ignition of landlordism, and the associated turbo-charging of the housing market, that furnished the fundamental basis of the broader national economy of the present. Housing matters beyond the dimension of economic transaction, and thus housing movements matter, too.

Tenant organising is done best when it is done sincerely – that is, for its own sake. For decades, a common mistake has been to use the low-hanging fruit of people's misery as a recruiting tactic or brand-building exercise. While there is of course a need for political education and bringing together different strands of struggle, it does a tremendous disservice to tenants to dip into their lives without any intention of committing to resolving their housing issues in the longer term.

The most striking features of groups like HASL are its longevity and dedication. HASL members have developed incredibly useful local knowledge about, for example, the council housing allocation rules and likely behaviour of local authority officials. Their longstanding experience of dealing with private-sector landlords has given their members a sense of what works and what does not. Successful housing groups have worked hard on this, to build effective organisations. Effective groups also know their limits, and help people to identify other options when something comes up that is beyond their abilities. Housing is very complex, and those with general activist experience can often cause more harm than good if they dabble in it.

Perhaps the most egregious example of this unserious brand-building 'activism' was the dispute in Camden behind the 1939 lawsuit that established that rent strikes are illegal. Reading between the lines, it seems that the disastrous Camden rent strike might have been intended as a recruiting operation for the Communist Party. The Camden flats had been organised with the help of the St Pancras Tenants' Defence League, which had recently held a successful rent strike in a neighbouring street, and which had strong Communist Party links. The landlord sued two of the tenants for all the missing rent, and won. The League ended up sticking two of its new recruits not only with ruinous personal liability for the estate's rent, but with a legal precedent that might well confirm that rent strikes are illegal (it has never been tested).[25] Quite the act of solidarity.

This fiasco was not necessarily characteristic of Communist Party organising in the 1930s, however. Many Communists were sincerely dedicated to organising in housing, anti-fascism and the connections between the two. In his memoir *Our Flag Stays Red* Communist Party MP Phil Piratin described how organising estates around housing issues had been critical in galvanising east London's working class in the run-up to the Battle of Cable Street. The Communists were essentially trying to outshine the British Union of Fascists – who were trying to recruit the very same residents – by making themselves useful on the housing front.

But this was bona fide organising on an ambitious scale, rather than a series of point-scoring stunts. The Communist-aligned Stepney Tenants' Defence League was a highly professional body that called and won high-profile rent strikes, and fought not just for tenants' basic rights but for rent *reductions* to which the tenants had no legal right. When its members at Southern Grove in Mile End, for example, demanded a rent reduction and the landlords pleaded poverty, 'the tenants said "we will take over the whole place and run it ourselves". The tenants got their rent reductions.'[26] Second only to Clydeside, this sort of practical radicalism in the 1930s represented the high point of housing organising in Britain. A system of tenants' committees, as well as more formal organisations like Stepney's League – many of which were organised under the auspices of a National Tenants' Federation – were often very effective. Piratin credits the strength of this movement, together with the recent memory of Cydeside in 1915, with the strong rent controls that were introduced at the start of the Second World War.[27]

For a time, the lessons of the dangers of organising for political recruitment seem to have been well learned. Incidents like the debacle of the Camden lawsuit – and the bitter betrayal of a high-profile St Pancras rent strike in 1960, when the strikers' Labour Party 'comrades' won the next council election and broke their promise to lower the rents – led the housing movement to reject representative politics. By the late 1960s, 'Tenants from every estate demanded that their organisations be "non-political" . . . The slogan "No Politics" was a reaction against party politics and a means of protecting the self-activity and independence of this particular struggle.'[28]

This independence is useful and important, particularly in an environment where councils bear so much responsibility for housing issues. Even nominally left-wing administrations, hamstrung by defunding and inhumane national legislation, are often responsible for carrying out acts of surprising cruelty, and tenants' movements continue to have a necessarily fraught relationship with party politics.

One of the things that anyone involved in housing learns very quickly is that virtually everyone has a sophisticated understanding of the housing question. These problems are so prevalent in our lives, they call so much attention to themselves, that people tend to think them over quite carefully. It was probably for this reason that, at the height of the pandemic in May 2020, Labour's short-lived shadow housing secretary Thangam Debbonaire wandered into a PR nightmare. With an eviction crisis looming, Labour announced that it favoured a policy of requiring tenants to repay pandemic-related rent debt over a two-year period, and Debbonaire claimed that writing off arrears would be a very 'un-Labour' approach.[29]

This provoked an immediate backlash. The idea that landlords should be uniquely shielded from the financial consequences of the pandemic, or that there would be room in anyone's household budget to top up their rent payments with yet more rent payments over two years, was obvious nonsense to pretty much anyone who had ever signed a tenancy agreement. But it was the intensity of feeling that seemed to catch the Labour Party off-guard.

In other words, the solutions are already in our neighbourhoods. No one needs to be persuaded about how bad things are, or how unjust. Our task is basically to gather the strands together. This is happening already, of course, with palpable effects. Campaigners in England and Wales have managed to wrest a promising Renters Reform Bill from an extraordinarily right-wing Conservative government. In Scotland, groups like Living Rent have won rent freezes, and a similar campaign claims to be close to victory in Northern Ireland. In places like Manchester and Bristol, and up and down the country, local groups are opposing gentrification-led development projects. There were particularly commendable acts of community protection during the pandemic, with some London estates successfully taking on landlords of pantomime villain–style wealth and malignance.

The movement will have two crucial roles in the years to come. First, there will be a pressing need for mutual support over the next few years, as the housing crisis begins to resolve itself in necessarily dramatic and violent ways.[30] Second, if the government abolishes 'no-fault evictions', as it has long promised, housing organisations will need to devote themselves to unpicking the extraordinary degree of rental discipline that has been established over the last few decades. Securer tenancies will undermine the silent compulsion behind the current system of rent-ratcheting, but not as an automatic consequence: landlords will need to unlearn their sense of power and expectation, and renters will need to seize the corresponding gains. This process will take time, energy and knowledge, but it is an exciting prospect.

Mike Davis reminds us about the prosaic nature of political organising: 'Unlike the broad-chested heroes of proletarian novels or Eisenstein films, rousing their workmates into rebellion with a single fiery speech, the classical rank-and-file organizer was more like a patient gardener constantly weeding daily plant life of its inevitable dissentions and jealousies.'[31] We will, no doubt, see many more patient gardeners in the coming years as the housing crisis drags on. But that, of course, is ultimately how we will win.

5

Illegitimate Concerns:
Race and Housing

Every day we see signs of the advancing tide . . . There is a special new statute there which imposes on the local authority a duty to house you. They must either find you a house or put you up in a guest house. 'So let's go to England,' they say. 'That's the place for us' . . . I trust the councillors of Crawley will keep their [feet] dry against this new advancing tide. I would dismiss this appeal.

Lord Denning, giving judgment in the Court of Appeal, December 1980

This book has laid much of the blame for the current housing crisis at the door of the wholesale reform of housing law that took place in the 1980s. But the radical new laws of the Thatcher era did not come from nowhere. Tenancy reform had been mooted in Conservative circles for years beforehand, and the ground was then laid by a high-profile Royal Commission. It had been set up by parliament to examine the poor conditions of working-class housing, and to arrive at the conclusion that deregulation was needed in order to attract investment capital. The Commission was led by, of all people, the consort of the then-monarch, the Duke of Edinburgh.

Prince Philip was, of course, well known for his racist comments. He regularly volunteered his personal views, putting his strong sense of racial superiority on display. In a certain sense he performed a useful role by exposing the racism at the heart of a colonialist nation: in many other places, such outbursts might have disqualified him from having a public say on the issue of working-class housing. Not so in Thatcherite Britain. The duke was instead given prominent roles in the social housing sector. Indeed, one of his many wretched headline-grabbing comments ('There's a lot of your family in tonight') was made at the expense of Atul Patel, the chief executive of a major social landlord, at an event where 400 British Indians had gathered to mark the state visit of India's president.[1]

It is disappointing that Britain has such a dearth of good, accessible writing on race and housing. In the United States, it is possible to buy two or three good books on the question of African-American mortgage lending alone. There is a great deal of literature exploring how land use throughout US history has led to the yawning racial wealth gap that exists today. It is perhaps an unfair comparison, given that housing policy in the United States has often been so extravagantly racist – for example, the New Deal–era policy of 'redlining' African-American neighbourhoods and then starving them of resources on the basis that they were dangerous or undesirable, while simultaneously funding mortgage investment in white areas. Racism in Britain can sometimes be better disguised. But we need to be much more clear-eyed about the racism that underpins and complements our own housing crisis.

Geographer Danny Dorling, in his 2014 book *All That Is Solid*, convincingly debunked the myth that the housing crisis was simply a case of too many migrants making unfair use of scarce resources. His argument chimes with the overall theme of this book: that supply discussions are something of a red herring. Indeed, in a context where homeowners are disproportionately white, and the vast majority of owner-occupied homes are underoccupied, it is very difficult to make a case that it is the migrants who are causing housing scarcity. If anything, the reverse is true.

Still, there is a deep-seated sense that racialised people in general – not just migrants – are the problem. Time and again, both the law and society exhibit an attitude as to who is or ought to be entitled to land and housing, and this attitude is then put into practice. The result is wildly disproportionate housing outcomes. This came into particularly sharp focus during the coronavirus pandemic: a 2020 parliamentary report identified a wide range of housing-related adverse health consequences for BAME communities (their term). It included the staggering statistic that one in three Bangladeshi families live in overcrowded housing, which is roughly double the proportion of black African households and *sixteen times* the proportion of white British households.[2]

Thus, we can confidently describe the housing situation in Britain as 'racist' within the definition put forward by American scholar Ruth Wilson Gilmore: 'the state-sanctioned and/or extra-legal production and exploitation of group-differentiated vulnerability to premature death'.[3] As we will see below, black and brown people are indeed dying disproportionately and prematurely as a result of housing conditions, even as property generates such enormous amounts of wealth for others.

Law, Race and Empire

I recently defended a social housing tenant in a complex antisocial behaviour case. My client was a black single parent with disabled children. She accepted that she had committed a serious act of antisocial behaviour: she had brandished a kitchen knife at her neighbours, and had been convicted for it in the criminal courts. That conviction allowed the landlord to bring eviction proceedings on what are called 'absolute and mandatory grounds'. This is a type of case that is exceedingly difficult to defend. My client's explanation was that she was not some sort of unstable menace, but a quiet tenant who had simply had enough of the racist taunts of her white suburban neighbours. One day her patience had snapped. She had kept telling the landlord about the racism, but there was an institutional reluctance to take her claims seriously.

For one reason or another, a video recording that my client had sent to the landlord's lawyers had got lost in the bowels of their complicated case-management IT system. By the time the trial began, no one on the landlord's side had watched it. But we insisted that they should dig it out, and during a short break in the proceedings my opponent and I sat down to look at it together. It showed neighbours gathered outside my client's house making monkey noises at her. We went back into court and – on one of those rare occasions when the monotony of civil proceedings flares up into a Hollywood courtroom drama – I played the clip to the housing officer in the witness box, who was suitably dumbfounded. Everything my client had been saying was true. The housing association had sided with its white tenants, and had utterly failed a particularly disadvantaged racialised one. At the end of the trial my rather fussy defences – technical and procedural in nature – suddenly looked quite impressive, and the judge seemed relieved to have a legal pretext for dismissing the case.

My experience of the law is that practitioners, judges and public authorities tell themselves we live in a post-racist society. This is particularly true in the criminal courts, where upstanding magistrates seem to think that overt 'street' racism is either a thing of the past, or a rare and unacceptable transgression of the rules of polite society. That is not only untrue, as my client's case showed, but it also completely misunderstands how racism tends to work. The allegation here is not one of intentionality. 'There are racists in the world', argues sociologist Gargi Bhattacharyya,[*] 'and some of

---

[*]   While Bhattacharyya is, quite rightly, well recognised as a scholar and writer, I should also put on record their much-valued contributions to the social and political well-being of Housing Action Southwark and Lambeth.

them have profited through exploitation, but racial capitalism does not emerge as a result of a plan. No one maps out this programme and then enacts it. What we seek to understand is the place of racialisation in particular instances of capitalist formation', and we can certainly see racialisation in the processes of house-price capitalism.[4]

In *(B)ordering Britain: Law, Race and Empire*, academic lawyer Nadine El-Enany highlights the sophisticated ways in which the law bars the racialised poor from accessing wealth in Britain today. Such wealth includes both the riches that flow from home-ownership and the benefits of social housing: 'the making of Britain's modern infrastructure', she argues, 'including its welfare state, was dependent on resources acquired through colonial conquest'.[5] In other words, the racialised poor are excluded from the very wealth that was built on the strength of their own generational subjugation.

The law achieves this by producing and reinforcing powerful social attitudes towards race and entitlement. Legal migration statuses – citizenship, refugees, visas, rights to remain – all contribute to an environment in which 'racialised people are cast in white spaces as guests, outsiders or intruders, as here today, but always potentially gone tomorrow' (El-Enany again).[6] This transient status fosters a sense that racialised groups are undeserving of enduring land rights and wealth in Britain. It is almost a complete perversion of the practice of land acknowledgment, which is increasingly (and rightly) common in places like Canada and Australia, by which racialised aboriginal or First Nations people are formally acknowledged to have originally inhabited the land. In Britain a sense of nativism is used cynically to dis-entitle racialised people from land wealth, thus keeping them in the private rental market where they can continue to be economically exploited.

These socio-legal attitudes towards race and housing are deep-rooted. The early-modern housebuilding prohibitions described in Chapter 2 were also essentially racist in their aim. The urban population growth that the prohibitions sought to stem was in part – although a part that was doubtless exaggerated in the public imagination – due to an increasingly established Jewish community from the 1650s onwards, as well as Huguenot and Dutch migrants. In fact the 1656 local petition opposing the 'private lucre' sought by the developer of Lincoln's Inn Fields complained that, if more houses were built, 'the poore of their parishes [are] like[ly] to be much increased; sundry papists, forainers, and lewd, idle and wicked persons harboured amongst them'.[7] Indeed, the very concept of an 'alien', as distinct from a legal 'subject', first arose in the context of property rights, rather than border enforcement per se. The Alien Act 1705, for example, established that land owned in England by Scottish nationals should be treated as foreign-owned property.

But the nadir of the racism–housing-law nexus did not come for another 300 years. Theresa May's 'right to rent' scheme was introduced under the Immigration Act 2014 as part of her 'hostile environment' regime. The scheme prohibited landlords from renting out homes to people whose migration status did not include a newly invented 'right to rent', and required landlords to carry out immigration checks under threat of criminal penalties. The new law was challenged in the courts by a migrants' rights charity, and their case was supported by various bodies that even included the National Residential Landlords Association. That was because everyone – landlords included – recognised that the scheme might lead to discrimination. Indeed, the courts accepted that the evidence showed that some landlords did discriminate against British people with 'ethnically non-British' attributes ('such as name, colour and accent'), and the challenge initially succeeded – though the result was overturned when May appealed.

The Court of Appeal highlighted the wide 'margin of appreciation' that international anti-discrimination laws confer on domestic governments, particularly when it comes to matters of national policy. The courts should, it said, generally defer to elected representatives when it comes to working out where to strike the appropriate balance. In essence, the Court said: 'Parliament really wants to do this, and because it doesn't necessarily require *all* landlords to behave in a racist manner, we're not going to stand in Parliament's way.'[8] It was not wrong about legislators' strong desire to see the measure in place. Despite the hung parliament that had been elected in 2010, this manifestly racist law passed with a Commons majority of nearly 300, because all but six Labour MPs abstained. Diane Abbott and John McDonnell were among the six who voted against, and Jeremy Corbyn spoke against the Bill and acted as teller for the 'no' votes.

The important point about the 'right to rent' scheme is not that it created racism in the housing sphere, but that it fostered and exploited pre-existing tendencies. It was law and society working in tandem. The state was harnessing a capacity for private individuals to police people based on their race – but it was a capacity that was already present. The policy sought to promote racial discrimination into an explicit and universal legal obligation, rather than a personal aberration by the worst type of landlords. The state knows from long experience that race and housing are intertwined, and from time to time it encourages such prejudice and tries to use it to achieve its policy aims.

But there was a sophistication to the policy – a novel element. Theresa May and her enablers on the Tory and Labour benches were so committed to the 'hostile environment' regime that they would not even allow migrants to be economically exploited for rent. Landlords – except for the most bigoted – were keen to receive rent from them; migrant tenants themselves were willing to pay, no better options being available – but the government preferred to see them homeless and deported than allow that economic activity to take place. By 2014, even the right to be exploited by landlords had been reserved for certain national and racial groups.

As far as race and housing-as-capital are concerned, Bhattacharyya has argued that 'techniques of racialised exclusion, division and differentiation continue to play a central role in the practices of capitalist exploitation'.[9] There are many examples of this, even on the crudest and most obvious level. Just nine days after the Grenfell fire, the *Independent* ran a story recording some local people's dismay that victims from the burned-out estate might be rehoused on an exclusive new development nearby. It had recently been announced that sixty-eight socially rented homes would be made available for Grenfell families in the luxury Kensington Row development, but some complained that 'north Kensington [where the fire had taken place] is not this Kensington'.[10]

This attitude drips with class- and race-based prejudice. It exposes an ideology about who is entitled to what land, and an anxiety that housing-based wealth should be protected from perceived threats, even in moments of extreme need. The racialised poor find themselves segregated and vulnerable in order to protect the value of other people's assets. When we hear that thoroughly British phrase 'There goes the neighbourhood', we know instinctively what it means in terms of race, house-price capital, and the relationship between the two.

Homeownership

In 1960s Britain, when 27 per cent of metropolitan landlords openly barred black and brown tenants and just 6 per cent welcomed them, many migrants and racialised people sought to buy property as a means of achieving housing security and avoiding a 'colour tax' in the form of higher rents for lower-quality housing.[11] A 1965 government report documents both the South Asian and black Caribbean communities setting up community lottery schemes to finance homeownership. Members would buy in, and each month or fortnight a member would 'win' and be awarded the whole amount that had been raised. This might pay for the initial deposit, or possibly even the whole house. An arrangement of this kind is dramatised in Sam Selvon's 1965 novel *The Housing Lark*.

But even those with money to spend were cheated and abused by an endemically racist system. Black and brown first-time buyers were frequently sold a pup: homes that were due for demolition; homes that were already occupied by secure sitting tenants; buildings so dilapidated that they were beyond economic repair; or simply – in the words of the government report – 'rubbish sold dear'.[12] Sellers either exploited recent migrants' lack of awareness about the idiosyncrasies of property-buying, or lied to them outright. Mortgage lenders, too, saw an opportunity for profit, targeting low-waged migrant workers with exorbitant interest rates and short-life second mortgages.

These practices served only to fuel the very prejudices that had caused them in the first place. Finding that it was impossible to service the mortgages or carry out repairs, some of these cheated new homeowners resorted to the very worst forms of landlordism to avoid financial ruin. They let out rooms at high rents, overcrowded their houses, and bothered any sitting tenants either accidentally (by surrounding them with overcrowded new neighbours) or on purpose (to persuade them to leave, in order to re-let). This then created a moral panic: 'an ingrained fear and apprehension, whether rational or irrational, inspired by the coloured landlord'.[13]

While, in proportional terms, white landlords were just as likely to carry out those sorts of abuses, a stereotype emerged of black landlords buying up property and menacing their elderly, white, rent-controlled tenants. In reality, many of these landlords played a crucial, if morally ambiguous role by accepting black, brown and migrant tenants when white landlords would not; but in the public imagination they were reviled not only for their 'sweating' practices, but for their gaudy displays of wealth. They had dared to succeed on British property-owning terms, and this was a transgression.[14]

While some have argued that the early 1960s saw a 'tacit consensus between the political parties not to "play the race card" in such a way as to exacerbate racial tension', it is clear that race was the centrepiece of political discourse when the housing crisis exploded into public consciousness with the Rachman scandal.[15] There was plainly a political desire to have an argument about immigration. Responding to a *Panorama* broadcast about Rachman in the House of Commons in 1963, the housing minister Keith Joseph openly admitted both that the capital's population had in fact been falling dramatically and that a huge number of new homes had recently been built – but he somehow still managed to blame housing profiteering on a shortage caused by 'immigration from all over the world, especially from the Commonwealth'. 'Extra people', he argued, 'however worthy, must sharpen the pressure on housing' – and he claimed that it was precisely this confected housing-shortage worry that was at the heart of government thinking on border enforcement.[16] Joseph cited the 1962 Commonwealth Immigration Act, which had controversially restricted rights of entry from the Commonwealth and then paved the way for the further immigration controls of the following decades, as the offspring of this hollow housing-supply panic.

The 1964 general election was then sullied by a race-and-housing row when the Conservative candidate for Smethwick distributed leaflets with the infamous phrase: 'If you want a n***** for a neighbour, vote Labour', and unseated the Labour incumbent. In 1965 the report of the Milner Holland committee on Rachmanism was launched, the *Daily Express* reporting that the chair had asked the press conference, 'Which do you prefer, snakes or shrunken heads?' – a plainly racialised allusion to some of the (black) landlords' scare tactics that the committee had uncovered.[17]

Enoch Powell's 1968 'Rivers of Blood' speech centred on an anecdote about the deleterious consequences that had apparently followed when a house in Coventry was sold to a black person. Powell's tall story invites us to sympathise with a white landlord who has paid off her mortgage and refuses to rent out rooms to black tenants, rather than with her new black neighbours. In other words, if there was an attempt by the political parties to avoid a race row in the early 1960s, it did not work: race, homeownership and immigration were instead inextricably linked in the public consciousness.

But my purpose here is not to decry the unacceptable racism of a bygone era. While the 1960s is a very clear example of El-Enany's argument about the symbiotic relationship between border regulation, societal racism and the withholding of wealth from the racialised poor, homeownership has long-term, generational socioeconomic effects – particularly in a post-Thatcher context in which housing assets are the main driver of prosperity. Official statistics show that white British people are still significantly more likely than average to belong to the club of wealth-perpetuating property owners.

In fact, this problem is getting worse: for younger generations (under thirty-five), white people are almost twice as likely to own as non-white people, whereas the gap for older generations is much narrower.[18] Low and falling relative levels of black and brown homeownership are bound to exacerbate racial wealth gaps with the passage of time. But this is not just a passive process, with consequential effects on racialised households. A 2021 report by the Runnymede Trust and CLASS examined the connections between gentrification and the 'churn' of the racialised poor: gentrification does not just involve the displacement of often-racialised poorer residents to drive up property values – it relies upon it.[19] Housing wealth, the cornerstone of the national economy and ideology, is very often predicated on whiteness.

Social Housing

Racial division was also foundational to the twentieth-century municipal housing project, not simply its unintended by-product. 'What was the use', asked Liberal Unionist MP Cathcart Wason in a 1903 debate on social housing, 'of spending thousands of pounds in building beautiful workmen's dwellings, if the places of our work-people, the backbone of the country, were to be taken by the refuse and scum of foreign nations?'[20] Six years later, the House of Lords tried to introduce a legal provision to ensure that municipal housing would be 'occupied exclusively by the working classes', and the mechanism they proposed was that 'other things being equal, the local authority shall give priority to applications made by British subjects belonging to the working classes'.[21] The House of Commons rejected that proposal on the basis that the matter should be 'left to the London County Council'. For its own part, the LCC itself was toying with the idea of barring those who were not British subjects from its social housing in the 1920s.[22]

In 1976 the Wilson government introduced the ground-breaking Race Relations Act to prohibit discrimination in employment and the provision of services, and also to establish the Commission for Racial Equality – eventually replaced by the Equality and Human Rights Commission. The Commission immediately carried out a number of high-profile investigations into racially differentiated decision-making by local authorities' social housing allocations departments, and uncovered the unequal way in which different groups were being treated, even in an era of greater formal legal equality. A remarkable amount of social-engineering power was concentrated in the hands of patrician local authority officers, the best of whom were cautious about race relations on mixed estates while the worst simply promoted white interests. 'Many state-sponsored attempts to generate communities out of strangers in

shared residential spaces', argues historian Sam Wetherell, 'operated with an implicit expectation that these communities would be
mostly or entirely white.'[23]

At worst, black and brown people were excluded from social
housing altogether. Partly out of a nativist concern that those with
an established local connection should be prioritised, and partly
out of an economic desire that the cheap labour of Commonwealth
migrants should be mobile rather than fixed, the 1960s in particular
saw a disproportionately high number of white households being
accommodated in council housing. Later, as historian of municipal
housing John Boughton explains, 'the [Greater London Council]
had informally based their allocations, in the words of one housing
officer of the time, on "an assumption that black and white would
rather live separately from one another"'.[24]

The Pepys Estate in Lewisham, for example, became a white
estate, while Milton Court, a mile away, was predominantly black.
There are many other examples of social-housing segregation
across the country, but Lewisham is a particularly striking example. Les Back's study of the Pepys estate shows how – blighted by
unemployment and social deprivation – it gained a reputation for
racist violence as it 'sank', and racialised minorities (who were
among the only people willing to accept housing there) 'invaded'
the once-thriving community. 'For the first three decades after the
war', argues Wetherell, 'new council estates were agents, sometimes unwittingly, in the reproduction of white supremacy.'[25]

The original thinking behind social housing was that it should
be, if not quite universal, very much in the mainstream. However,
the leitmotif of this book has been the way in which the law –
however well meaning – interacts with economics to change
behaviours and produce complex consequences. In 1977 the government brought in the first laws obliging local authorities to
accommodate certain vulnerable classes of homeless people in
council housing. This encouraged an ideological shift towards the

'residualisation' of social housing provision: it only existed for people with the most extreme needs.

Increasingly, from the 1970s onwards, legislation sought to ensure that council housing was allocated based on need: an option of last resort for those who particularly merited help from the state. Again, a change in the law sowed the seeds for social discontent. As stocks fell and council housing became increasingly scarce, and as state policy treated it as being increasingly non-mainstream, fashionable thinking began to emerge that estates were hotbeds of crime and deprivation. High-density urban estates – particularly those where local authorities had placed black and brown households – became 'sink estates' or 'difficult to let'. The self-fulfilling nature of this prophecy was obvious to anyone who bothered to think about it even from the very start. In 1977, *Race Today* complained that 'the allocation of families to "sink" estates, which white families will refuse, will continue, as will the forcing out of black families from their homes, by racist whites'.[26]

As well as providing yet another proof of El-Enany's theory – that the spoils of colonial conquest, in the form of social housing, are withheld from the racialised poor – the social engineering of council housing tenants had far-reaching social consequences for the tenants themselves. Again, these were obvious from the start. Another *Race Today* article, from 1975, cites the campaign demands of a group of Bengali squatters in east London, who were refusing to be sent to the white estates a good distance away from their local area in the East End, and were instead squatting empty municipal properties. 'By sending Bengalis into places like the Canada Estate in Poplar, you have exposed us to racial attacks and our children to isolation in schools, where the local children have not yet been taught that people who do not speak English are not culturally backward.'[27] It must therefore be acknowledged that there was at least some basis to the local authority officers' concerns about mixed estates – although the solutions should have been obvious from the community's demands (in essence: 'house us in the East End, where we are already squatting in your buildings').

This 'residualisation' of council housing continues to intensify. In 2014 the coalition government granted police-like powers to social landlords, allowing them to take their tenants to court and have them sent to prison for antisocial behaviour on housing estates, which is probably the very last thing that black and brown tenants need. At the time of writing, the Grenfell Inquiry was drawing to a close and, while the eventual report is likely to contain a great deal of useful material for anyone interested in race and housing, it is already clear from the parties' submissions that the horror of the fire was part of Britain's colonial legacy.

The total indifference to the safety of Grenfell's residents – from national and local government, and from the private firms involved in working on the tower – has been staggering. It is no accident that the tower itself was so explicitly racialised: among its pejorative nicknames were 'the Moroccan Tower' and 'Little Africa'. As journalist Peter Apps puts it, 'On 14 June 2017, Grenfell Tower – a building named after a former colonial leader – was covered in combustible plastic and filled with a community who traced their family or personal history back to countries conquered by Britain in the two centuries before.'[28] Just eleven of the sixty-eight* residents of the tower who died were white, and even they included people from Ireland, Portugal, Spain and Italy.

But as a counter-current to 'residualisation' – as access to social housing improved for non-white applicants, and allocations began to reach relative parity – the social housing sector has become subject to a pincer movement of underfunding and increasing commercialisation. In 2021 Croydon Council carried out an internal investigation into its failings following an ITV News report

_____

* The official death toll was seventy-two, but four of those were visitors rather than residents.

about a four-year water leak at one of its homes. It found that a lack of resources meant its repairs team was about 50 per cent under-staffed. Morale was low, expertise was lacking, and repairing services were focused on 'firefighting', leading to dreadful living conditions for many of its tenants. The report notes that Croydon is an area where the majority of people – 53.1 per cent – are from black, Asian and minority-ethnic backgrounds.[29]

As global majority people came to access social housing in greater numbers, a growing concern developed about housing associations losing sight of their social purpose. The sector is becoming exposed to profit-seeking. In other words, the racialised poor have only been admitted to social housing on the condition that they transfer their wealth – in the form of rent – to the private capital that has been attracted to the increasingly deregulated sector.

Apart from the web of events that led to the Grenfell fire, the point is best made by the tragic death of a two-year-old child in Rochdale, Greater Manchester, in 2020. Awaab Ishak lived in a housing association property and died from a respiratory condition caused by exposure to mould in his home. The landlord, Rochdale Boroughwide Housing, had been receiving complaints since 2017.

Among a litany of failings and sins of omission, the landlord's staff had blamed the mould problem on 'lifestyle issues', including claims that 'ritual bathing' involving a 'bucket' was taking place – an allegation they had never even asked the family about. As specialist housing lawyer Giles Peaker puts it, 'that tired racist allegation . . . gets trotted out with pretty much every complaint of damp, or raised as an accusation where there is a leak into the flat below, where the tenant is African' – although there is also some suggestion that it is somehow derived from suspicions surrounding Islamic prayer ablution practices.[30] Campaigners from Greater Manchester Housing Action point out that Rochdale Boroughwide

Housing's CEO received a pay rise to £170,000 while the housing association was carrying out the very failures that led to Awaab Ishak's death.

Renting

The victory over landlords through the introduction of rent controls in 1915 has its own complex relationship with race. In January 1918 in Glasgow Harbour, Britain's first 'whiteness riot' took place. The very same union leaders who played a now-legendary part in Red Clydeside's housing struggle – most notably Willie Gallacher – had also sought to marginalise black and Chinese colonial workers, and the ensuing tension culminated in armed violence between seamen. Outnumbered, a group of black (British) sailors from Sierra Leone fled, with a growing crowd of white workers in pursuit.[31]

The question that confronts us when we look at the private rental market of today is how it compares to the 'colour tax' system in the 1960s, by which racialised people – when they were able to find willing landlords at all – were faced with higher rents for lower-quality housing. In an era of sophisticated anti-discrimination laws, by which the processes of racism are challengeable in the courts, is the private rented sector still racist in the sense that it produces group-differentiated vulnerabilities?

The most obvious answer is that landlords do still exhibit even the crudest and most unlawful forms of discrimination. In 2017 the Equality and Human Rights Commission brought court proceedings against Fergus Wilson, who – together with his wife Judith – was at one point one of the country's largest buy-to-let landlords. Wilson had sent an email to his lettings agent saying: 'no coloured people because of the curry smell at the end of the tenancy'. The EHRC won, and Wilson was ordered to lift his prohibition.[32]

Wilson is perhaps not your average landlord. A bizarre character, at the time of writing he had recently been defeated in heavy litigation brought by a Kent local authority to try to stop his four-year campaign of 'repetitive, frequent, oppressive and offensive correspondence' with the council, which included writing to a local councillor and telling him that he would 'serve the people of Ashford best by committing suicide'.[33] But given the vast proliferation of landlords (see Chapter 3), and given the prevalence of racism in contemporary Britain, the odds are excellent that Wilson is not unique. A 2022 study by Heriot-Watt University found that one in three black people who had experienced homelessness had also faced racial discrimination from a landlord.[34] The government's own evaluation of its 'right to rent' policy showed that one in five landlords admitted to being aware of racial discrimination in private renting in the geographical area where they operated.[35] It is naive to suppose that the EHRC can protect people from attitudes like this by bringing the occasional lawsuit.

Even where racism in the private rented sector is better disguised or more nuanced than Wilson's, it remains very effective. For decades, there has been a widespread prohibition on renting to Housing Benefit recipients – a policy that tends to be known as 'no DSS', after the long-defunct Department of Social Security. The housing charity Shelter and my colleague Tessa Buchanan have recently had several successes in establishing through the courts that individual cases of 'no DSS' were illegal because they had disproportionate and unjustified consequences for tenants with disabilities. But black people, too, are nearly twice as likely to receive Housing Benefit as white people (14 per cent versus 8 per cent), so the still-common practice of stipulating 'no DSS' is bound to have disproportionate effects in terms of race.[36]

Even where landlords themselves are not the problem, the private rented sector throws up all sorts of barriers. The massive increase in shared housing among younger people in recent years, coupled with severe competition for rooms, means that the right to housing is increasingly in the gift of the housemates themselves. Generally there are no formal criteria for selecting housemates, and it is frighteningly easy for racist attitudes and behaviours to disguise themselves as idiosyncratic preferences. Lettings agents' practices, too, are likely to create problems. It is common, for example, for agents to require a guarantor, who generally needs to be a UK homeowner. Given the gulf between the proportions of white and non-white homeowners, the effects of this will be felt disproportionately, and particularly among migrant households.

Perhaps the most invidious form of racial disparity is found in the ever-increasing tendency towards gentrification and dis-placement. As the Runnymede Trust and CLASS report cited above makes clear, the racialised poor on insecure private tenan-cies are far more likely to be subject to the 'churn' that takes place when areas are redeveloped for profit. For all the racist and anti-migrant tropes to the contrary, when we look around our towns and cities it is obvious that wealthier, whiter people are the ones who are 'invading' and taking other people's homes. 'Homeless-ness has grown massively in BAME communities', notes Kevin Gulliver of LSE's Human City Institute, 'from 18% to 36% in the last two decades – double the presence of ethnic minorities in the population'.[37]

In 2022 Shelter and the *i* newspaper carried out research into the private rented sector, and found that racial inequality is 'hard-wired' into the housing system. Rents are indeed more expensive, as a proportion of income, for BME renters (the term used in the report). BME renters were significantly more likely to have been subject to a rent increase of more than £100 per month, and were also more likely to be 'constantly struggling' to pay.[38] Housing journalist Vicky Spratt also notes the disproportionate distribution of 'housing stress' across racial groups.[39] While a great deal of this is due to structural factors and the intersection between race and class, rather than 1960s-style bigotry, the fact remains that black and brown people transfer proportionally more of their wealth to asset-owning landlords than white people do, while also facing greater insecurity and worse conditions.

It is ironic that the person who has come closest to meaningful policy change since the 1980s is Michael Gove, whose role in mainstreaming Islamophobia and whose rejection of the MacPherson Report's acknowledgment of institutional racism in the Metropolitan Police suggest that he was very unlikely to have the best interests of minoritised groups at heart. But even Gove's proposed reforms to the private rented sector are likely to benefit racialised people last and least. Elsewhere in this book, the decline and elimination of the sector have been presented as an unequivocally good thing. But if this were to happen, it would undoubtedly be migrants and the racialised poor who would suffer first and most severely. Many would continue to be priced out of homeownership – and as long as social-housing allocation rules include requirements for an enduring 'local connection', there will be barriers to access for recent migrants, particularly those with irregular migration statuses.

For many, private renting is the only realistic option. Rent controls, too, mean that newer arrivals will have to pay the highest rents. Racist housing outcomes are so ingrained that even those of us who want to see change must acknowledge that our own actions and campaigns are bound to have racist consequences.

Anti-Racism and Resistance

One almost has to admire the unashamed cruelty of the 'right to rent' scheme – almost. It is designed in a way that makes it nearly irresistible. In the 1970s, the government had introduced a racially targeted policy that 'all black people applying for benefits or insurance cards should be required to produce their passports as part of the witch hunt against "illegal" immigrants'; Keith Joseph, once again, was the minister responsible. But members of the Civil and Public Services Association trade union, later the PCS, tasked with enforcing the policy refused to comply.[40] Theresa May's scheme puts the burden of compliance on a non-unionised, deeply atomised and politically reactionary group (private landlords), and backs it up with the threat of criminal penalties against them. It is genuinely difficult for anti-racist action to be effective in such circumstances.

But housing has traditionally been a proving ground for radical resistance, and that is certainly true in the case of anti-racism. In the British context, Madden and Marcuse highlight a 'wave of rent strikes in London's East End in the 1970s [which] was part of Bengali antiracist politics and black radicalism in Britain', as well as the anti-fascist housing organising that had taken place in the 1930s.[41] In fact, this Bengali movement had sprung from the 1975 mass-squatting protest mentioned above. Supported by the Tower Hamlets Squatters Union and the *Race Today* Collective, the Bengali squatters formed an organisation, called BHAG, which stood for Bengali Housing Action Group, but also means 'tiger' in Bengali and 'share' in Urdu and Hindi.

By 1977, BHAG had gained a degree of clout. 'Tony Judge,' *Race Today* reported, 'at that time Britain's largest landlord, in his position as Chairman of the Greater London Council's Housing Management Committee, found himself forced to sit at a negotiating table with Bengali workers.' What Judge was told was informed by BHAG's sharp and radical analysis. 'For years, the British state has bought immigrant labour on the cheap, dodging the necessity to house, to skill and to reproduce the black labour force', said *Race Today*; 'BHAG is a rejection of the solution to housing problems that the state has posed . . . a restricted and restricting amount of hostel accommodation – a solution which reduces the black worker, as in Germany and other parts of Europe, to a wage labourer with no rights in the society and no claims on decent housing.'[42]

BHAG and *Race Today* saw the harm that had been done by the social engineering of local authorities, but they sought to weaponise it. 'Our demand that we be housed where we are many arises out of our own realisation that "ghettoes" are our source of protection and strength, in the present racial climate of Britain, and provides the base [from] which we can launch our attack for decent housing.' As well as deliberate ghettoisation, the authors may have been mindful of policies like that of Birmingham, where the local authority had sought to disperse recent migrants into white suburbs by trying to impose a rule that no more than one in six tenants in any given building could be black.[43]

Race Today's thinking about adopting housing concentration as a source of strength is far from outdated. Tottenham's Broadwater Farm, for example, has been frequently castigated as a dangerous 'sink' estate by the government. But Tice Cin, an artist who grew up in Tottenham, writes:

> After the 1985 riots (though we call it an uprising) police spoke of feeling thwarted by the layout of the estate, their frustrations revealed in local blogs, internal reports and news segments. That frustration became a point of local pride, because it was a single form of relief against the over-policing and surveillance that targeted individuals in the estate, especially young Black men.[44]

Owen Hatherley notes, too, that when Broadwater Farm was renovated, 'its black residents had far more say and control over the estate than they ever did in its alleged heyday, and by the 21st century they had successfully created a valued, popular and successful working-class community'.[45]

In the days after the Grenfell fire, I spent some time with the survivors volunteering at the community's Law Centre. I was a deeply shocked and angry young lawyer. Long before I became aware of the estate's totemic status as a vestige of colonialism, I wrote:

> Standing near the tower just before last week's candlelight vigil, it was clear that this was a community that cared for itself. Older children from the estate were checking up on each other, making sure they were getting by and arranging to meet later. Neighbours were giving out fruit to the people who had come to stand in solidarity with their community. People were standing on stairwells and balconies to hear the speakers. If this community has even a fraction of that spirit under ordinary circumstances their sneering new neighbours in luxury flats are lucky to have them.[46]

That spirit did endure. The community went on to pursue a magnificent campaign for justice, highlighting the racism at the heart of the disaster and making the case for better housing for everyone.

Cui Bono?

In 2021, to much self-congratulation, the Johnson government passed the Domestic Abuse Act, which it described as a 'once in a generation opportunity' to support victims of domestic abuse. However, as the Public Interest Law Centre pointed out, 'despite high-profile campaigning and lobbying . . . amendments to the act requesting the removal of the NRPF condition* for all abused women, the establishment of safe reporting mechanisms, and the extension of eligibility and time frames for the Destitution Domestic Violence Concession were all voted down by Parliament'.

PILC describe how one of its migrant clients had been forced, as a result of the pre-existing legal framework, to stay in a home with

---

* 'No recourse to public funds' is a legal migration status that prohibits a person who is entitled to remain in the UK from receiving any state support.

her abusive partner for months before she managed – with exceptional good fortune – to obtain a place in a refuge.[47] The government is content for the law to allow migrant women to suffer gender-based violence rather than change its housing policy.

The current framework of housing law was not just sanctioned by a racist duke; its policies were forged in the context of riots in Brixton, Toxteth, Handsworth and Moss Side in 1981, and on the Broadwater Farm Estate in 1985. The point about race is that it is not bolted on to other, more fundamental considerations: it is crucial to understanding the housing crisis. Housing wealth is so often defined in terms of its apartness from racialised people, and race is fundamental to the system of house-price capitalism described throughout this book. Ours is a society that evinces a persistent attitude that black, brown and migrant people are not entitled to the benefits that flow from good housing.

House-price speculators are not only loath to share their neighbourhoods – they see a need actually to remove the racialised poor altogether, through gentrification, as a means of protecting or increasing the value of the asset they are concerned with. A society that bases its prosperity on homeownership, and at the same time sees an ever-increasing gap in ownership levels is practising white supremacy. Like the divide between 'generation rent' and 'generation rentier' described in Chapter 3, the entrapment of black and brown people in the private rented sector represents a perpetual transfer of wealth from the racialised poor to the class of disproportionately white homeowners.

Such is the heritage of colonialism and imperialism. Property wealth was built on the successes of those projects. As British surveyor George Head put it on the eve of the First World War: 'it is evident that any check to our supremacy in trade cannot fail to have a downward bearing on property values'.[48]

6

Everything Everywhere All at Once: Local Housing Crises

For this vast city is like the head of a rickety child, which, by drawing to itself the nourishment that should be distributed in due proportions to the rest of the languishing body, becomes so overcharged that frenzy and death unavoidably result.

Scottish political writer Andrew Fletcher,
commenting on London in 1703

While there is an overwhelming tendency to think about the housing crisis in metropolitan 'alpha city' terms, all sorts of different-looking crises have been springing up all over the country. When I lived in Manchester, around the start of the global financial crisis, about 11,000 people lived in the city centre; by 2024 that population is expected to pass 100,000.[1] Inner Manchester is opening new primary schools to meet demand, while many London boroughs are being drained of their schoolchildren as housing costs force families outwards. In Liverpool, the council devised a scheme for selling dilapidated terraced homes for £1 to stop empty buildings from rotting away.

In rural Cornwall, rapacious demand for holiday homes is starving the local population of affordable places to live. In Burnley, security grilles define whole streets of empty terraced houses on sale for £12,000 each, while – just yards away – security gates keep wealthier homeowners and their properties safe from harm. In Edinburgh, AirBnBs exacerbate scarcity and wreck the urban social fabric. In countless commuter towns and villages, new housing developments lead to anxious conflicts between vulgar housing crisis analysts, who treat new supply as the inevitable goal while also disdaining its effects on communities.

It is important to acknowledge the overwhelmingly dominant focus that London receives. A number of books are published every year about the London real estate phenomenon, but it is fairly difficult to get an accurate sense of what is happening even in major cities like Leeds, Glasgow or Bristol without talking to residents and activists directly. This chapter explores just a few of the regionally idiosyncratic housing crises that have been unfolding all over the country, many of which are completely different from the pattern familiar in south-east England. Not only is it impossible to discuss every part of Britain in this chapter; the various hyper-local phenomena are so numerous and unique that I could not possibly claim to know about more than a fraction of them. For readers living in Devon or Dundee, Blackpool or Bangor, I hope that the arguments outlined here offer a useful framework for analysing local circumstances, even if they are not specifically mentioned.

But, for all of my earnest commitment to exploring what is happening outside London and the south-east, the capital looms large in any conversation on this topic. As the epigraph that opens this chapter illustrates, it is virtually impossible to discuss the rest of the UK without defining it against London: a chapter about regional housing crises that refused to mention London would be Hamlet without the prince. I am afraid, therefore, that there is no relief from the capital even here.

Levelling Up

In housing-lawyer circles, the West Midlands town of Telford has become a byword for the long-distance displacement of homeless people by urban local authorities. It is usually mentioned as the butt of cynical jokes about the dumping of social-housing applicants. I was at an event recently where a mention of Telford was serving its usual purpose during a speech, and a local-authority-side lawyer heckled the speaker with the remark that it was actually a very nice place to live. 'Very well, then,' retorted the speaker, 'a barrister in the audience has just volunteered to swap her house in London with the next homeless family from Camden that's sent out to Shropshire.'

Established as a new town in the early 1960s, Telford opened its doors at a particular moment of economic decline, and – despite local industrial development in the 1970s – unemployment in the town tended to far exceed the national average throughout the late twentieth century. Many of its first council tenants were placed there as 'overspill' by Birmingham council, and this is a mechanism that has built up a new head of steam in recent years. Freedom of Information requests in 2020 showed that London councils sourced more than 20 per cent of their temporary accommodation in other regions of the country (often in the Midlands). By 2022, an ever-increasing number of local authorities outside London were adopting the practice of shunting people to areas with cheaper housing.[2]

At the most basic level, housing wealth tends to be determined by its proximity to productive capital. Where wages are higher, better rents (even monopoly rents) can be extracted, and housing values will tend to follow suit. Prices for housing land shot up, for example, in new urban sites right across the country during the industrial revolution, as towns and cities boomed and the new urban working class became trapped in the housing-commodity market. But the story of Britain's subsequent deindustrialisation is well known. As Tom Hazeldine explains in *The Northern Question*, deindustrialisation saw wealth and productivity concentrated increasingly in south-east England, and on the eve of the pandemic 'average household wealth ranged from £170,000 in the North East (mostly pensions) to £450,000 in the South East (a mix of property, pensions, stocks and shares)'.[3]

The question of why poor housing conditions cannot be improved by simply making homes better, regardless of local economic conditions, seems to have genuinely stumped many policymakers, as we can see from their attempts to deal with the issue. For discussion of the muddle-headed 'Pathfinder' project of the Blair era – an attempt to address 'failing housing markets' in deprived regions by making homes fancier – see Chapter 2.

But this thinking was by no means new. As far back as the 1860s, the government pursued an agenda that it called – hauntingly – 'levelling up'. The intention was that city-centre slums could be improved if waged workers were to move to better housing in the suburbs, and that this would ease crowding and squalor in town, as only the destitute would remain. But waged workers needed to be where their jobs were, and in many cases the flight to the suburbs did not take place even when overcrowded districts were demolished as a means of sending them on their way.[4] The suburban homes by themselves were incapable of attracting wealth. In the 2020s, the government re-adopted 'levelling up' as its mantra, and made it the centrepiece of a new Department for Levelling Up, Housing and Communities. A White Paper announced that 'the government's ambition is for the number of non-decent rented homes to have fallen by 50% [by 2030], with the biggest improvements in the lowest performing areas'.[5] They also intend to 'invest in more homes in the North and Midlands to relieve pressure on the South East'. It does not seem to occur to the government to ask *why* cheap rented housing is in a poor condition in the 'lowest performing areas', or *why* – regardless of the many homes already in existence in the North and the Midlands – there is such intense demand for housing in the south-east. Houses in parts of County Durham sell for just 110 per cent of the national average salary, but building more of them is unlikely to help.

Even though millions of people struggle to afford their housing costs, we do not all move to small towns in County Durham. Housing is not a pure consumer choice. It is affected by all manner of things, but principally work and economic activity: people are either tied to where they are, or they need to follow jobs and economic prospects. As a result, prices will tend to remain lower in parts of County Durham as long as wages and rentable values are comparatively low there. Drawing on Marx, David Harvey explains that 'prices form which reflect production conditions at diverse locations under varied conditions of concrete [i.e. specific] labour'.[6] Nearly 10 million people continue to live in London, despite the fact that average house prices are eleven times the average salary.

These sorts of disparities expose the folly of the ideological shift that took place in the 1980s. Before then, governments tended to disdain any 'excessive' profiteering based on property speculation. This was not a moral standpoint but an economic one: over-investment in landed property diverts money away from industry and other, properly productive activity. Governments that are concerned about the welfare of domestic capital prefer to see money invested in business. But British government policy changed under Thatcher. It began with the perhaps understandable desire to attract investment into a fairly squalid private sector, but coincided with a project of reducing manufacturing subsidies and relocating employment to southern England. The astonishing outcome was eventually made clear with the quantitative easing programme after 2008.

It soon became apparent that most of the money that central banks had intended to pump into the economy through QE had actually ended up in housing values in the south-east, rather than in businesses. Hazeldine points out that 'the first three years of QE saw house prices jump by 17 and 15 per cent in London and the South East, compared to rises of 2 and 4 per cent in the North West and Yorkshire-Humber respectively. In the North East, prices didn't move.'[7]

The nightmare of the pre-Thatcher governments had come true – money that was intended to boost the real economy had ended up sitting idle in land holdings – but nobody seemed to mind. By 2010, house prices in the south-east had become a stand-in for a national economy proper. Doreen Massey argues that, after 2008, the government and private capital began to 'share an under-standing of London/the South-East as the golden goose of the national economy', and their task was to 'explain to the rest of the country how and why the widening inequality between regions can be beneficial to all'.[8]

In this sense, the fostering of the London housing market has been an aspect of Britain's deindustrialisation. By the early twenty-first century there was no longer anything else productive to invest in. South-eastern property values became the focus of government attention. The other regions were encouraged to emulate the ideology and practices of house-price capitalism as best as they could, or were assumed to somehow benefit from London's largesse when they could not.

It is, of course, relatively easy to understand how policymakers managed to get things so wrong. House prices are the great British success story. It would be selfish indeed to deliberately restrict such a miraculous source of prosperity to the capital, and Homes England is currently working on 'Kings-Cross-style' redevelopment projects in twenty towns and cities in the hope of sharing the wealth. It remains to be seen whether places like Wolverhampton, a beneficiary of the project, will manage to match King's Cross, which has attracted the UK headquarters of Google. But even the logic of the model is bizarre: its architects hope to take places that do not currently have an affordability problem and make them more expensive. Tellingly, the scheme is supported by housing developers like Wates, who delight in plans to 'redirect [state] funding towards homebuilding in the Midlands and the North'.[9] At best – if this works as intended – it would be disastrous for people who live there; at worst, it would be an expensive experiment in creating the aesthetic indicators of prosperity outside south-east England in the hope that prosperity itself will somehow follow. In a country as uneven as Britain, any attempt to 'level up' the nations and regions through house prices alone is Potemkin economics.

Urban Studies

Anyone who thinks that massively boosting new supply is the solution to a crisis of housing costs would do well to take a walk through central Manchester. From Ancoats and New Islington to Trafford, encircling the city centre, masses of new housing has sprung up in the last ten years. The central population has exploded, out of all proportion to national population growth. The result is that estate agents' windows now show rents and prices comparable to London's, while tensions simmer about the social cleansing of working-class inner suburbs. The underlying problem has only been exacerbated. There had been concerns among developers that 'record-breaking years of development between 2016 and 2018 could flood the market', but a mystified *Financial Times* reported instead that 'as the new-builds have gone up, so have sale prices'.[10]

Manchester's housing crisis is one of the closest in format to that of south-east England. A regional centre of wealth and finance, it has followed a model of chasing affluence by raising property values as quickly as possible; but there are important differences between the north-west and the south-east. Manchester has seen a series of conscientious development efforts by the state and capital, in contrast with London's relatively passive method of watching the value of all existing buildings shoot upwards regardless of how much new housing is being built.

Owen Hatherley has described Manchester as 'a flagship for urban regeneration', and it is difficult for the most generous reader to interpret that as a compliment in the context of a deepening housing crisis.[11] Interestingly, research on the financialisation of housing in Greater Manchester shows that about 44 per cent of housing across developments in Manchester and Salford is privately rented, which indicates a booming 'build to rent' phenomenon (traditionally absent from the British new-build market). It is this new, often rented, accommodation that is driving the increasing unaffordability of the city and surrounding region.

In other words, the current housing crisis in Manchester had to be invented, because it was not happening as spontaneously as in London. Rent lies at the economic heart of this problem. Marx and Engels (who both spent a good deal of time in Manchester) would be proud.

Manchester is the headquarters and proving ground of quirky developer Urban Splash, who – as Hatherley puts it – 'excelled at selling neoliberalism as radicalism' by framing property development as counter-cultural.[12] At the time of writing, Google's Street View images for New Islington are dominated by builders' hoardings covered with Urban Splash's logo. Go and have a craft beer on the canal, though, and you can now see the new buildings in real life. The developer's logo has been replaced with those of Manchester Life (an institutional landlord of Abu Dhabi origin) and Homes England – the former selling its wares to well-to-do tenants; the latter revelling in the simple fact that homes have been built, regardless of the consequences for the city. The fig leaf of radicalism has been torn away.

While Engels was describing Manchester's appalling living conditions, housing reformers

> frequently argued that if only the working classes could be persuaded to devote a rather larger proportion of earnings to accommodation the scarcity of houses in many areas would be solved by the operation of market forces . . . Such arguments were usually linked with a condemnation of housewives for mismanagement and of their husbands for drinking, gambling and other unnecessary expenditure.[13]

This was a time when working-class rents were about 10 per cent of household income – a fraction of what we spend today. In reality, our generation has indeed been persuaded to devote a much larger proportion of our earnings to rent, and yet even in places like Manchester we are still lectured about inadequate housing supply and profligate household spending. We are still blamed for the deepening housing crisis that government and capital have confected.

Manchester, of course, is not the sole contender for second-city status. Birmingham lays claim to this title, as do the national capitals of Scotland and Wales. What unites them, though, is the way in which their housing circumstances have fallen into line behind London in recent years. Hazeldine's point about quantitative easing failing to benefit northern England ten or fifteen years ago no longer holds true. It was not London but the rest of the UK that saw the sharpest growth in unaffordability during the pandemic. Savills reported two years of 'unprecedented growth' outside the capital – 16 per cent over two years in 'prime regional' areas after 2020. The staple media reports of people fleeing London to get more for their money in some charming, run-down-but-exciting provincial city are becoming alarmingly scarce as the housing crisis spreads and intensifies.

Edinburgh – like Scotland more generally – is blessed with the sharp analysis and effective member-support of Living Rent,

Scotland's tenant union. While Living Rent capitalises on the pearl-clutching concern about short-term lets that flares up each year for the Edinburgh festivals, and makes the point that housing stress exists not only in August, the group has a shrewd understanding of the landlordism that drives the Scottish housing crisis more fundamentally. The group's manifesto makes the point that council housing sales and the buy-to-let boom continue to drive ever more tenants into poverty. It recognises that the housing crisis would not cease to exist if AirBnBs were banned overnight. It calls not just for rent controls, but for legal rent reductions. Its success has, in British political terms, been sensational: in 2022 the Scottish parliament passed legislation freezing rents, and the Scottish equivalent of assured shorthold tenancies was abolished in 2017. What distinguishes groups like Living Rent, though, is the scale of their ambitions. Political successes that are unimaginable in the rest of Britain are treated as insufficient: nothing short of full rent controls and replacement of lost social housing will do.

Edinburgh's experience over the next few years is going to be particularly interesting. In Chapter 1, we saw how the mere threat of strengthening rent regulation sent Blackstone scurrying from new investment in Berlin. And the argument throughout this book has been that the extraordinary rent-raising capacity of the assured shorthold tenancy regime is the driving force of housing wealth, and of the housing crisis more broadly. Scotland has abolished insecure tenancies and temporarily capped rents – and yet the rental market is going from strength to strength.

In the first quarter of 2022, analysts reported an 'unprecedented' year-on-year rise in rents of 14.2 per cent.[14] As many in the tenants' movement in England argue, tenancy reform alone will not stop the constant rent-raising that defines the housing crisis. The effects of unpicking the Thatcherite housing framework will probably take some years to make themselves felt. It took about thirty years for the housing crisis to ramp up, as landlords slowly developed behaviours that reflected the economic powers baked into short-term tenancies. Likewise, it is likely to take some time for an increasing number of stable tenancies to produce dampening effects on price, as rental discipline breaks down and tenants learn and implement their greater sense of power.

This is especially true in Edinburgh, where prices in the private rented sector continue to be affected by the yearly churn of the city's massive student population, which mimics the quickly rising rents of insecure tenancies. But Scotland's cities will be very interesting to watch in the coming years. Groups like Living Rent will have a critical role to play in supporting their members through the pain and hardship that tends to occur as housing markets adjust to new economic realities.

Forgotten Places

One of the pleasures of being a courtroom lawyer is that I get sent all around the country to argue cases. I have passed through many of England and Wales's more arcane towns, and I have developed a fairly specialised knowledge of the routes between railway stations and courthouses. When I was a trainee I was sent to a particularly obscure *palais de justice* in Mold, Flintshire, which is a few miles inland from the North Wales coast. I had gone to argue about the amount of damages in a low-value claim, and my opponent – sensing my youth and inexperience – tried to hustle me into settling the case. He claimed he could win a vastly inflated sum for his client. But when I refused, and we went into court, his extravagant arguments about the serious nature of the matter were interrupted by the judge: 'Mr Smith', he said, 'you're reading from the wrong expert report. Perhaps you've picked up the wrong case file by mistake?' I had been warned by my colleagues about the hostility with which 'London counsel' tend to be treated by the regional judiciary (and this is often well deserved), but as my opponent tried to recover his composure, the judge warmly wished me a very safe trip back home.

I say 'London counsel' deserve a degree of hostility partly because barristers are, as a rule, insufferable, but mainly because London lawyers are often out of tune with the rest of the country. We have become battle-hardened and aggressive from our daily dealings with extremely hard-pushed urban local authorities. I am often genuinely surprised by the change in tone and practice when I am instructed in an out-of-London case. In Wales, for example, where housing is a delegated matter, housing policy is leagues ahead in terms of its humanity. That is partly because the Welsh administration has not been as aggressively right-wing as the Westminster government, which sets England's laws, but that is not the only factor.

For London councils the difficulties are so acute that it is virtually impossible to be a 'good' housing officer: staff are under enormous pressure to make adverse decisions. I am often acting in cases against London local authorities that seem to prefer incurring the costs of fighting and losing a court case rather than giving someone the housing they need. This may be – and I don't know because I am not privy to those decisions – because the litigation works out cheaper than the housing.

The story of the UK is often told in terms of geographic inequality: a yawning chasm between the metropolitan and the provincial, with almost mythical origins. Apart from the bright spark of the industrial revolution, when British regional industry was world-leading, the 'vast head and languishing body' dichotomy is the favourite narrative – that is, when anyone bothers to talk about the UK outside London at all.

This is certainly a tale that chimes with the post-2008 recession. With the exception of Manchester's conscientious property boom, throughout the 2010s housing conditions were governed by the fact that it was northern England, Wales, Scotland and the Six

Counties that bore the brunt of austerity. Tom Blackburn notes that 'in London, any economic slowdown was soon shrugged off, as the local economy grew by 17 percent from 2010–14, compared to growth of 3–4 percent in the Northern English regions and 1 percent in Northern Ireland over the same period'.[15]

In Liverpool, for example, a gold-rush of city-centre housing development had been taking place just before the global financial crisis hit. This was despite the fact that, as Lily Gordon Brown explains, Liverpool already had a surprisingly low population density as a result of its late-twentieth-century decline: 'the city region's land mass is largely empty, as are many of the buildings that occupy it'.[16] What happened next, in the distinctive argot of a local letting agent, was that 'the market literally fell off the face of a cliff'.[17] Shiny new buildings in the city centre sat empty, or were let to students at well below their intended prices.

Empty developments in regional towns and city centres defined the wake of the financial crisis. Nick Clegg launched a 'Northern Futures' initiative, which included a scheme designed to 'see abandoned buildings brought "back to life" in a renewed effort to tackle a chronic problem where vast sites in Northern cities become empty and unused for so long that whole areas can become blighted'.[18] Even in 2016, by which point talk of a 'housing crisis' or even a 'housing shortage' had become ubiquitous, the number of empty homes in places like Bradford was actually growing.[19] Low incomes, low demand and low rents were leading to poor housing conditions, as even basic maintenance became uneconomical.

This post-2008 phenomenon echoes similar economic disparities throughout modern history. Hazeldine points out that when the Great Depression struck in the 1930s, 'its worst and more enduring effects [were] felt in industrial monotowns well away from the stockbroker belt, in what was otherwise a good decade for consumers and wage-earners'.[20] Meanwhile, as discussed elsewhere in this book, London's renters were busy organising. And in the late nineteenth century the successes of imperialism in producing goods abroad had had a massively depressing effect on British agricultural regions: 'A man such as Lord Pembroke, for instance, found that by 1896 his outgoings on his agricultural estates were exceeding income; only his urban ground rents in Dublin kept him going' (while, from a modern or an Irish perspective, Pembroke was merely resorting to one form of colonialism to escape the effects of another, it is notable that at a time of crisis he had to resort to metropolitan housing wealth).[21]

A 2019 academic study found a correlation between 'leave' voters in the 2016 EU referendum and areas where housing markets were declining or stagnating. The model corrects for coexistent factors like unemployment rates, pay gaps, local migration levels, and divisions of age and social class. 'Where house prices are low (£100,000)' the study concludes, 'owners have a 59% probability of voting for Brexit and non-owners around 54%, whereas where prices are high (£750,000) homeowners have dropped to just 37% probability whereas non-owners have dropped only to 44%'. This tendency cut across regions: Brexit voters, it was found, were not concentrated in particular places, but they were united by the fact that they were homeowners who, because of Britain's regional disparities, had been excluded from the spoils of house-price capitalism. The research applied the same method to France, finding that poor house-price growth coincided with support for Marine Le Pen, which the authors treated as a similarly 'populist' phenomenon.[22] Before the referendum, Doreen Massey had noted that, when it comes to issues of intra-national housing inequality, 'we rarely get to vote about them directly'. The 2016 vote is perhaps the closest we have come to doing so.[23]

But, at the risk of putting a modern twist on a traditional tale, very recent trends are interesting. The 2021 census showed that housing affordability had worsened in almost all – 91 per cent – of local authority areas in England and Wales. The census data tell the story of the housing crisis, and it is such a striking tale that the team at the Office for National Statistics (ONS) has made an interactive animation of their affordability map. Starting in 1997, virtually the whole country – including London – is shaded in pale yellow, indicating a price-to-salary ratio of just four- or five-to-one. Press play, and the major cities gradually shade to green and blue throughout the nineties, London always being the darkest spot (reaching a price-to-salary ratio of eight- or nine-to-one in 2000).

By the mid 2000s virtually the whole map turns green and blue, with the darker tones of southern England spreading like rot. In 2008–09, in the wake of the global financial crisis, the regions turn pale again: suddenly, housing wealth is more obviously concentrated in the south, and this continues for the next ten years. In 2021, though, housing affordability begins to worsen significantly right across England and Wales. The ONS concludes that, by the 2020s, 'Only 16 local authority areas in England and Wales had affordability ratios of five or less, compared with 27 in 2020, and 270 in 1997.'[24]

Rural housing costs had begun to grow faster than urban ones, with average countryside house prices overtaking average city prices during the pandemic, and then increasing their lead.[25] If this book had been written just a few months earlier, the story would have been yet another one about the distressed regions failing to recover, but the new narrative must be that nowhere is safe from increasingly challenging housing costs. London is everywhere.

The post-pandemic boom outside London has sometimes been called the 'race for space'. A basic analysis presupposing increased demand and a buoyant property market would have us believe that people are dispersing themselves all over the country in order to face the very unaffordability they are supposed to be fleeing in the first place. Again, a simple Marxist understanding of this price phenomenon is more fruitful. Land values are higher when they are nearer to sites of employment. Housing costs differ between locations mainly because there are differences in access to wages and employment opportunities: areas with higher wages allow landlords to extract higher rents. But a series of lockdowns and a growth in the feasibility of working from home seem to have taught us that we can now demand higher housing costs in places that were previously treated as being too remote.

Writing on the political economy of housing in the 1970s, Marxist commentators argued that there was a tendency that 'employment opportunities become more and more concentrated, while those seeking to live near them increase in numbers', and increased housing values become concentrated in affluent cities as a result. Advances in transport infrastructure had periodically offset that tendency, spreading housing wealth outwards; but, fifty years ago, it was difficult for the authors to conceive of new technology that would perform a similar role.[26]

But technology does advance, and the sudden, necessary adaptation to off-site working is beginning to have profound effects on the economics of land. As well as a collapse in demand for office real estate, we appear to be seeing something of a reversal of the tendency of housing wealth to be concentrated in the south-east, as ever more parts of the country are treated as being within reach of sites of higher-paying work. People have fled the extravagant costs and poor conditions of housing in the cities, but retained their income, while landlords and house-sellers nationwide convert this excess wage into higher rents and prices. You could live in Margate and earn a London wage, which gives Margate landlords a licence to charge London-like rents. By this method, the crisis of housing costs is bursting its usual banks.

The electoral success of the Conservative Party in 2019 appears to have been achieved by unifying a constituency of homeowners. The expansion of homeownership since the 1980s had not only contributed to a restructuring of class identities, but had had the tangible economic effect of offsetting stagnant wages and austerity. And electoral data appear to show that the 2019 election result was derived from a 'traditional – if regionally distributed – Tory voting bloc' of homeowners, including many outright owners.[27] In other words, the current government benefited from lower house prices outside the south-east because those prices had allowed a sufficiently large number of people to afford to buy their homes, and many of them ended up voting Conservative.

But if that argument is correct, the Conservatives face a growing difficulty. The problem with diffusing house-price growth across Britain – spreading it to economically poorer regions – is that it prices an ever-larger number of people out of the club, shrinking the electoral bloc that rallied to the Conservatives' banner in 2019. It is difficult to know how the government will respond to this across-the-board house-price growth. Will it encourage the economic benefits, at the expense of pricing people out? Or will it try to curb regional price rises? If so, how will it manage that while keeping its traditional south-eastern voters' assets intact?

Genuine Scarcity?

Even in popular, rural, geographically demarcated places like Cornwall, the prohibitive cost of housing cannot fairly be blamed on a lack of existing buildings. Cornwall has long been a dark spot for affordability on the ONS's interactive map. But journalist Taj Ali reported in 2021 that

> there are just 52 houses available to rent in Cornwall listed on the Rightmove website. In contrast, Airbnb, the popular holiday rental site, boasts over 10,000 active listings in Cornwall. In fact, there are as many live Airbnb listings right now as there are council homes in the whole of Cornwall . . . In 2020, there were nearly 12,000 households on Cornwall Council's housing waiting list.[28]

In other words, the social housing waiting list could be almost eliminated if the existing buildings were somehow repurposed. This is unlikely to happen, however, as long as it is more profitable for landowners to use homes as short-term holiday lets than as regular housing. And, in tandem with producing genuine scarcity in some places, the economic effect of Airbnbs more broadly is to cause the potential yields of housing to surge, driving up local rents and housing costs across the board. In fact, given the newfound mobility of housing wealth, and the cautionary experience of central Manchester, building more (non-social) homes in Cornwall is very likely to make things worse.

For years, the housing crisis followed its traditional model of two waves moving in opposite directions. Where there was wealth, prices were high; where there was deprivation, there was squalor and abandonment. The left-behind places, on the one hand, were deprived of the asset-value inflation on which so much of the nation's wealth had been built; but, on the other, they tended to be spared a serious crisis of affordability. In terms of price increases, south-east England is now being outperformed by just about everywhere else. The dilemma that faces us now is that housing is becoming too expensive everywhere.

7

The House Always Wins?

Now, you're able to work
for a living,
And rejoice in your strength and your skill,
So try to be kind and forgiving,
To a man whom a day's work would kill.
You can work and still talk to your neighbours,
You can look the whole world in the face.
But the landlord who ventured to labour,
Would never survive the disgrace.

'Pity the Downtrodden Landlord' (trad.)

In 2017 I was representing Paula in a homelessness dispute with her local council. Paula, her partner and their two children had been evicted when they had been unable to meet the rising rents in the private sector, and the council had to provide them with temporary accommodation. This accommodation – for a family of four – was a converted shipping container, which had been installed, along with a number of others, on a strip of vacant concrete behind a parade of shops near Greenford, a post-industrial suburb near the fringes of west London. It was blisteringly hot in the summer and freezing in the winter, the metal was hazardous, and it lacked any privacy. The family's rent was just short of £1,600 per month, or about £19,000 per year. What this shows us is that by 2017, a shipping container in outer London, when used as a housing com-modity, produced more revenue than many jobs would have generated in wages: a teaching assistant would have been paid (on average) £16,556 for working full-time that year.

The family – a working household – had been unable to find their own place to live. The situation had deteriorated so much that the state had to step in not just to find them accommodation, but to pay dearly for it, too. And this extortionate rent repre-sented something near the bottom end of the private rented sector. The council was not paying that horrifying rent for a brand-new and well-fitted home – not a city-centre new-build, or even a modest suburban flat – but a shoddy unit of temporary accommo-dation provided to a homeless family as a temporary expedient. The state was providing more 'passive income' to the family's landlord than many employers would pay to the same household in wages.

In *The Housing Question*, Engels argued that it made little sense to talk about a 'housing crisis'. He reasoned that housing is always a serious problem for the working class under capitalism – conditions are invariably poor, and it is never easy to pay the rent; and that periodic flare-ups of concern only take place when the sit-uation deteriorates to the point where the middle class begins to be affected. But it must be supposed that even Engels might concede that what we are seeing today is both extraordinary and unsustain-able. Housing costs are out of all proportion to the productive economy. If a capitalist society can no longer sustain its useful poor, then it is, by its own standards, in crisis. Like all crises, the housing crisis must at some point come to an end. The question that con-cerns us in this chapter is what the end of the housing crisis might look like.

Can't Pay? We'll Take It Away!

Ten years before this book was published, Danny Dorling wrote that 'the cost of housing cannot continue to rise as incomes and benefits fall'. This was in 2014, in the wake of the short-lived housing slump that followed the global financial crisis. Dorling went on:

> Predicting house prices can only be a very inexact science. But I place most faith in David Blanchflower's assessment that the housing price trend is still downwards in 2013. He is supported by the IMF, which says housing prices in the UK remain too high and could easily drop by a further 10%–15% relative to Britain's current average salaries, which themselves continue to fall during 2013.[1]

A decade later, during which housing costs have managed to make record-breaking advances as wages have continued to stagnate, anyone who predicts a housing crash is surely at risk of falling into the same error.

Why were commentators wrong ten years ago? And what would it take for this juggernaut to stop? We have already seen that the state has put an extraordinary amount of effort into keeping prices high through policies such as quantitative easing and low interest rates – but that is not a complete answer to the persistent rise in living costs over several decades. If it were simply a result of speculative investment, the housing market would be a bubble: a frenzy of anticipation where the amounts invested in the system were simply not justified by the fundamentals. But rented housing is, in fact, a profitable business.

Property website Portico.com produces an interactive map of rental yields in London, which is updated daily. At the time of writing virtually the whole city, with the exception of extremely highly priced areas like Mayfair, was showing a very healthy yield of around 4 per cent.[2] Similarly, research by the Council of Mortgage Lenders in 2016 found that the average rental yield was between 3 and 5 per cent, even after the downturn in 2008–09.[3] In other words, the housing market cannot properly be described as a bubble. Rents have consistently yielded a respectable profit, so the purchase price of housing has genuinely been justified.

The fundamentals of the housing market have been sound, and the price of housing is a true reflection of its productive capability as an asset. That is not to say that there are not dubious parts of the housing market: it is absurd, for example, that studio 'microflats' are being sold on the redeveloped Battersea Power Station site for more than a million pounds, and there are staggeringly expensive pieces of super-prime real estate in Britain.[4]

The ultra-high end of the market may well be as bubbly as vintage champagne. But at the more workaday level, the growing class of renters continues to justify the price of 'ordinary' housing assets by consistently paying the ever-higher rent, providing decent yields for landlords and house-price growth for homeowners. If and when the housing boom ends, it will not be because investors' confidence in a Ponzi scheme has suddenly snapped, but because the working class has.

As the *London Review of Books* has put it, 'In the absence of global meltdown or a collective Maoist turn by London's renters, politics remains the only remedy' to a system of wealth built on house-price-growth. Exciting as it sounds, this *bon mot* is probably not exactly right: a fourth option is a simple collapse in people's ability to pay their rent. As we saw in Chapter 1, residential rents, particularly urban rents, are not really subject to competitive forces – and, when left unrestrained by the state, they tend to reach monopoly prices. But the point about a monopoly price is that it is the maximum amount of money *that can be paid*. In a situation where, as Marx put it, 'the monopoly price creates the rent', the price is determined by the ability of the buyer (in our case, the average tenant) to pay. If a monopoly price can no longer be realised, one of two things must happen: prices will fall to the level that the buyer can afford; or society continues to meet landlords' demands, but socially acceptable housing conditions tumble as we are forced to compromise even further on the type of housing that those prices will command. We are at a fork in the road: Do prices fall to meet new financial constraints, or do costs rise as conditions continue to decline?

Back to Dickens

In the early 2020s in Britain, during the economic fall-out of the Covid-19 pandemic, and then the invasion of Ukraine, the political narrative has been dominated by discussion of a 'cost-of-living crisis'. Eye-watering levels of inflation have seen the prices of necessary goods and services increase at a runaway pace. Energy bills, in particular, rose to rates that would have been thought impossible a few years earlier: the spring of 2022 saw an average increase of £700 per household (a rise of 54 per cent on the previous year's bill), with another substantial rise taking place just six months later. Meanwhile, employers were imposing below-inflation pay rises, or real-terms pay cuts, which failed to compensate for these new spending commitments.

By the end of 2022, institutional investors like pension funds were showing signs of divesting from real estate.[5] The question, then, is what happens when landlords' demands for rent come up against the limits of society's ability to pay – when there is simply not enough flex in the average household budget to meet all of these new cost-of-living expenses on top of the ever-rising accommodation costs on which the housing economy is predicated.

Private renting in London had become so fierce that tenants began to be charged non-refundable deposits merely to book viewings for rooms – rooms they had only a small chance of securing. This was not because anything fundamental had changed about the supply and demand of homes in the city. There was no sudden or extraordinary shift in its population, nor in the amount of accommodation. Instead, London renters simply understood that they had to accept any new conditions that landlords imposed. Britain has an extraordinarily disciplined class of renters.

An important aspect of a monopoly price is societal acceptance of prices and conditions. Landlords had begun to charge viewing fees, tenants had begun to accept the necessity of paying them, and the idea that people could and would tolerate those fees became generalised. The same is true of conditions. The type of housing that people are willing to accept has declined rapidly – but there is the potential for things to get so much worse.

During the great 1880s London housing crisis, the Royal Commission on the Housing of the Working Classes found that 'rents in the congested districts of London are getting rapidly higher, and wages are not rising',[6] and that conditions were becoming correspondingly more squalid. In Hong Kong – given in Chapter 3 as a prime example of the tension between keeping land costs high and keeping wages cheap – the compromise that has now been reached is that more than 200,000 people live in boxed-off areas in subdivided flats known as 'coffin homes'. Hong Kong's tenants have come to accept appalling living conditions rather than forcing prices to fall. Los Angeles, similarly, seems to have acquiesced in a sudden and dizzying increase in the population of street-homeless people.

In Naples in the late nineteenth and early twentieth centuries, contemporary commentators 'marveled at the miracle of ever larger rents from the ever poorer and more wretched *fondaci* and *locande*', while living conditions sunk to abysmal depths.[7] During the same era in Mumbai, rents and land values trebled over a thirty-five-year period, while wages for unskilled workers rose by only 5 per cent, causing a massive intensification of the city's slums.[8] The question facing Britain today is whether its housing crisis can be pushed any further without breaking – whether conditions will become significantly worse, so that prices can be maintained, or rents will be forced to fall instead. If it is the former, Mike Davis's *Planet of Slums* (a taxonomy of modern-day urban squalor in rich and poor countries alike) provides a chilling range of possibilities.

It was in March 2023, while I was thinking through this gloomy prophecy, that I answered a call from London Renters Union organisers about a fire in a Shadwell flat, which had taken place two weeks earlier. The fire brigade had just released the flat, and there was a tense standoff between the landlord, the tenants and the police about who should be let back in first. The tenants were worried about their belongings (which they had not been allowed to see for a fortnight, and did not want the landlords to touch), while the landlords were concerned about photos and reputational damage.

We brokered a deal, and I watched as something horrifying took place: three local authority workers emptied a burnt-out East End slum. The three-bedroom flat was crammed with twenty beds. The tenants lived – by necessity – extremely neatly, and suitcase after half-charred suitcase was passed out from the tiny bedrooms while the skyscrapers of the Square Mile loomed over us a few hundred yards away. One of the residents – a forty-one-year-old father of two named Mizanur Rahman – had been sleeping in a bunk, and died from the fire. The time for prophesying about modern British slums had come and gone.

Here was racial capitalism *tout court*. Many of the smoke-spoiled suitcases still had their LHR luggage tags, as the residents – mainly delivery drivers and students from Bangladesh – had recently come to live in the lee of one of the world's most prosperous financial districts. According to one resident, they paid £100 per week for the privilege of living in such dangerous and appalling conditions. They had kept both the landlord and the city at large going, and yet here we were: bundling a dozen passports and wallets into carrier bags, marvelling at the number of lives that had passed through that front door, and wondering whether the suitcases we were carrying had belonged to the dead man. And of course, for all her hollow words about 'burning injustices', the phenomenon of migrants being forced into invisible, lethal slum housing can be laid squarely at Theresa May's door.[9]

Naturally, the building had been built by the London Borough of Tower Hamlets as council housing in the 1950s. The legal and economic conditions designed over the following decades had turned the flat from a site of hope and security into a cash cow, generating tens of thousands of pounds each year for the leasehold owner. And the estate backed onto Cable Street, which had been such an important site in the combined struggles against fascism and grasping slumlords less than a hundred years before. The neighbours and renters' union had organised a magnificent community response for the occupiers, but it is unforgiveable that we are having to fight these battles over and over again. We have to be prepared for things to get worse.

The Cost of Living

It was, troublingly, several successive years of falling wages that led to the end of the late-Victorian property development boom, and the massive Edwardian housing slump in which house prices fell by 40 per cent. A 1913 Board of Trade report (titled, ominously, *Cost of Living*) explained that the working and lower-middle classes in particular were having to spend less on housing costs as wages fell. Some fled to the suburbs, newly accessible by public transport, while other households were forced to double up in overcrowded accommodation, and all the while newly built housing sat empty.[10] Tenants simply could not afford rent rises as before. But at the same time it was difficult for landlords to lower rents to match this new economic reality, because the cost of servicing their own debts was increasing as interest rates and tax burdens rose. Housing was suddenly a liability rather than an asset.

While it is always lazy to rely entirely on historical precedents, and everything of course happens in its own unique context, the similarities between the Edwardian crash and the early 2020s are striking. At the time of writing, while things are very uncertain, almost half of UK households are worried about being able to keep up with rent or mortgage payments.[11] If landlords continue to raise rents as usual, will they come to find that people are simply unable to sign up to tenancy agreements on the terms offered? Or that they sign up, but eventually fail to pay? If so, will rents cease to rise, and will rental yields fall? Does the squeeze on living standards in the early 2020s spell the end of ever-rising rents? And if this is a crash in the Edwardian mould, will it also be of Edwardian proportions? Forty per cent of housing value is a great deal of money.

It would be an amusing but terrible irony if domestic energy prices were the final straw of the profit-driven housing crisis. As historian Sam Wetherell points out, one of the key ambitions of the project of building mass social housing that took place after the war was to bring a great many people out of the reach of the utilities markets. Local authority officials went on research trips, in some cases beyond the Iron Curtain, to borrow ideas for cutting-edge district heating systems, which collectivised energy supply on council estates and alleviated the cost of warming the home.

So revolutionary was the idea of the working class being able to afford to heat every room in the house that a reactionary campaign (the Women's Solid Fuel Council, sponsored by the coal industry) lobbied against central heating and in favour of the family cohesion generated by gathering round an open fireplace.[12] Sadly, a great deal of this modernisation project was later undone – both by the physical un-picking of communal systems under the Right to Buy sell-offs, and by the imposition of the market-based system of energy supply that so excellently typifies neoliberalism: laughably light-touch regulation, the whiff of price-fixing, and handsome profits for shareholders. We have foolishly exposed ourselves again to corporate energy prices, and made ourselves hostages to fortune – and *what* a fortune! – as the 2020s cost hikes have shown.

Finding the limits of monopoly prices in the rental market will not be a quick or straightforward process, but a slow, structural and deeply painful one. It will, no doubt, involve evictions for rent arrears or rent hikes, large-scale inability to find adequate housing, and a great deal of stress, worry, movement and sacrifice. While renters' dwindling incomes, on the one hand, will impose a downward pressure on rents, on the other hand the economic relationship between rents and house prices encourages landlords to keep rents high to justify the value of their investment.[13] The unstoppable force of an economy founded on rent rises meets the immovable object of wage restraint.

In the early stages of the Covid-19 pandemic, we saw how easy it was for the housing economy to thrive despite the phenomenon of falling rents in cities – and especially London; but this was a temporary blip rather than a proper readjustment. It posed no real threat to the overall structure of a system based on a generally fierce private rented sector. Similarly, housing recovered remarkably quickly after the downturn that followed the 2008 financial crisis. Just as it took decades for economic actors to develop a hegemonic understanding of the fact that the assured shorthold tenancy regime was a licence to increase rents, and for the housing crisis to ramp up as a consequence, it will very likely take a long period of structural change for this deep-seated behaviour and understanding to reverse itself. Rent discipline and the apparent natural law of constant rent rises will take time to break down.

In Scotland, for example, tenures akin to the English and Welsh shorthold tenancies have effectively been abolished, as Scotland has repealed its 'no-fault evictions' mechanism; but this did not lead to a sudden change in landlords' thinking. On the contrary: groups like Living Rent are still in a pitched battle against rising housing costs. The housing market is unlikely to wake up one morning and decide that the system is no longer working for landlords and house-price speculators, even if rents do fall.

But it is important to note that the current sharp shocks to household finances have come on top of more than ten years of austerity and wage stagnation, during which many people already sacrificed their living standards to meet their housing costs. Many renters have probably also reached their limit in terms of the type of housing they are able to tolerate, particularly as people have taken stock of their housing needs as working habits have changed during Covid lockdowns, and the need to be near physical sites of work began to relax. A generation of city-dwellers in their twenties and thirties are already living in shared houses without living rooms, or overcrowded family homes, with appalling and dangerous conditions and in inconvenient locations; there may not be much more that renters, as consumers, are able to forgo in terms of housing standards. Meanwhile, the state has also limited the amount that it is willing to pay in Housing Benefit.

As a result, the 2020s look set to see a battle royal between various household expenses. Prices – particularly monopoly rental prices – may adjust to reflect what the average renter is willing and able to pay. With the national economy based in no small part on steadily rising rental yields, and a cost-of-living-crisis in which people are genuinely worried about surviving, conditions have rarely been more auspicious for economic melodrama.

For the private landlord, 3 to 5 per cent is a perfectly respectable rate of return on investment – but it is also a relatively narrow margin, which runs the risk of being squeezed, eliminated, or even reversed. This may seem like a surprising prospect after so many decades of iron-clad profits, but owning land can be an expensive business. It comes with obligations to maintain and repair the buildings, which can be costly at the best of times. Buy-to-let mortgages are particularly sensitive to changes in interest rates, as around 85 per cent of them are interest-only.[14]

Hundreds of thousands of landlords are affected by the expensive scandal surrounding liability for dangerous cladding, which was attached to millions of buildings as a result of Britain's fatally flawed system of building regulation and control. The cladding scandal has also begun to expose the appalling build quality of many homes, which comes with expensive consequences for owners.

The government is making noises about replacing the system of assured shorthold tenancies in England and Wales with securer, less profitable ones. In Scotland, rent freezes have been imposed to help tenants with the cost of living. One does not have to feel sympathy for landlords to recognise that it would not take very much for profit margins to be eliminated.

It seems unimaginable to us today, but it was only sixty years ago that private renting was so unprofitable that landlords could not even afford to carry out essential repairs. In short, it is not impossible that the average landlord might see their profits disappear altogether. Some fairly small changes in the prevailing conditions would pose a very serious threat to the current system of rent-extraction.

Moreover, it is worth thinking about why the housing economy weathered the storm of the global financial crisis in 2008. As many have convincingly argued, a concerted state policy of attracting capital to housing by ensuring that interest rates remained low was broadly successful. Low or falling interest rates are crucial for boosting the value of housing, and this appears to have been true for more than a decade after the global financial crisis.[15] Low interest rates also helped individual homeowners who had fallen on hard times, repossessions peaking at just 0.43 per cent of all mortgages in 2009, compared to 7 per cent in Spain and 15 per cent in the United States.[16]

Interest rates are now much higher across the world. This has the obvious and well-known effect that mortgage lenders will raise their own interest rates, reducing homebuyers' means and constraining house prices. But rising interest rates also have the more profound effect of reducing house prices directly, according to the 'capitalisation' method explained in Chapter 1. A housing asset worth £240,000 when interest rates are at 5 per cent would be worth half of that – £120,000 – if interest rates rose to 10 per cent.

The financial crisis of 2008–09 also saw hundreds of billions of pounds of quantitative easing, which helped to ensure that sixteen months of falling house prices was followed by business as usual for rentiers and homeowners. But this tactic was running out of steam by the time of the pandemic. It relies on the Bank of England buying gilts; but the Bank, turning its eye to volatility in the broader economy, committed in autumn 2022 to an 'orderly end to its gilt purchase scheme'.[17]

In addition to that, the housing market would now represent a significantly heavier burden for monetary policy to shoulder. According to Savills, having spent the last ten years gaining £750 million in value *per day*, the total value of the UK's homes stood at £7.39 trillion in 2019 just before the pandemic arrived – up from about £5 trillion during the first quantitative easing programme.[18] Homeowners are bound to worry that monetary policy will not save them this time.

In short, if the next few years spell disaster for the landlord, and for their ally the homeowner, it will probably not be due to a Maoist turn, but a characteristically capitalist one. The contradictions of capitalism – its periodic frenzies of profit and crisis – will play their customary role. In the words of Patrick Jenkins in the *Financial Times*, 'as night follows day, bust in real estate markets follows boom'.[19] The question has only ever been: When? There will come a point when even a highly productive working class is unable to meet the rents demanded of it. And when urban rents actually *exceed* working-class wages, we are in dangerous territory.

It is possible that we will see a dramatic collapse, resembling the bursting of the property bubbles in, most notably, Ireland and Spain a decade or so ago, or the Edwardian crash. But it is just as likely that a collapse here would be altogether less spectacular and slower, given that housing investment in Britain is more deeply rooted – based more on the genuine productive capacity of residential land than the mere confidence of speculators. But the haunting examples of Spain and Ireland are worth reflecting on. In both countries, half-built shells and abandoned speculative construction projects – begun where there was financial backing but no actual need for housing units – litter parts of the landscape. What grim future awaits our built environment? No doubt the expensive new money-boxes in city centres will become very difficult to sell, and buildings – neighbourhoods, even – might lie empty: dark forms looming on the skyscape.

But what happens if a downturn takes place while these glass megaliths are still being built? As Marx pointed out, and as developers themselves are always at pains to emphasise whenever they are trying to dodge their 'affordable' housing obligations, house-building profit margins are often fairly small. It is the anticipated increase in land values that makes construction profitable. 'In cities that are experiencing rapid growth', Marx wrote, 'particularly where building is carried out factory-style, as in London, it is ground-rent *and not the houses themselves* that forms the real basic object of speculative building.'[20]

With that in mind, if rents fall, will luxury developments stand half-finished, like great Ozymandian tributes to a society led by a cult of rentierism? In fact Shelley's sonnet 'Ozymandias' was written in competition with another poet, his friend Horace Smith. Smith's poem, while much less stirring, describes an imagined London following a societal collapse. Whenever I walk past a half-built skyscraper in the ghoulish Vauxhall–Nine Elms–Battersea mega-development, I cannot help but think of its second stanza:

> We wonder – and some Hunter may express
> Wonder like ours, when thro' the wilderness
> Where London stood, holding the Wolf in chace,
> He meets some fragment huge, and stops to guess
> What powerful but unrecorded race
> Once dwelt in that annihilated place.

A Housing Market with an Economy Attached

For landlords, the consequences of a reversal in the fortunes of the rental market are obvious. When the wheels come off, deprived of their rental profits and the associated asset-price growth, the fifty-eight-year-old average landlord would be left with just their average non-rental income of £24,000. That whole class of 2.5 million people would see a sudden change in their fortunes.

But it is not just landlords and developers who would be affected. The financialisation of homeownership – the project of asset-based welfare, in which owner-occupied and tenanted homes are both treated as an equivalent for any other form of investment – is predicated on the profit-generating capacity of the rented sector. As Harvey points out, 'When trade in land is reduced to a special branch of the circulation of interest-bearing capital, then . . . land-ownership has achieved its true capitalistic form.' He goes on: 'Once such a condition becomes general, then all landholders get caught up in a general system of circulation of interest-bearing capital and ignore its imperatives at their peril.'[21]

What are those imperatives? What is the peril? As the government is so fond of impressing on us when it comes to *other* forms of investment: your capital is at risk, and the value of your investment can go down as well as up. To quote Harvey again: 'The integration of landownership within the circulation of interest-bearing capital may open up the land to the free flow of capital, but it also opens it up to the full play of the contradictions of capitalism.'[22]

Tribune columnist Joe Bilsborough has argued that the UK 'can at least be partially understood as a housing market with other parts of a modern economy attached to it'.[23] This is not as glib a comment as it may seem. The Office for National Statistics estimates that, in the midst of the Covid-19 pandemic, the rate of growth of household net worth – 8.4 per cent, or an extra £11.2 trillion – was only 'marginally below the pre-[2008] downturn average growth rate'. In other words, there was significant economic growth in the UK even at a time when the economy was more or less mothballed – and land-value increases, founded on rising house prices, were the biggest factor in that growth.[24]

Such sustained increases in land value have put Britain in a position in which more than half of the country's net worth is now made up of land values – approximately double the proportion of the net worth of Germany that is made up of land values. This is extraordinarily dangerous: it only reached as high as 40 per cent at the height of the Victorian housing boom in 1885.[25] The main part – the *absolute majority* – of wealth in the British economy is made up of a type of asset that everyone agrees will, at some point, fail.

At a certain point, the process that we saw over the thirty or forty years since the deregulation of the private rented sector may go into reverse gear. The value of homes could begin to fall significantly, as rents are forced down and yields are squeezed or eliminated. When landlords sell up, the ordinary housing market – to use the benign terminology of analysts and newspapers – 'cools', and competition between buyers lessens. Prices fall to reflect the new reality of rents, which not only fail to rise year-on-year – the fundamental assumption behind modern house prices – but may in fact fall to meet society's reduced means. At the other end of the market, and possibly at the same time, demand for ultra-high-end investment housing may well suffer due to rising interest rates. The extent of this decline is anyone's guess.

The problem, of course, is that we have bet our shirt on a rising housing market. The point about asset-based welfare is not just that housing wealth provides for individuals, but that their material well-being feeds into the wider economy. Writers like Matthew Watson and Colin Crouch have talked about 'house price Keynesianism' or 'privatised Keynesianism', in which mortgage debt and individual housing wealth is used to boost spending and stimulate the broader economy.[26] Whether or not that is precisely true, it is obvious that falling house prices, in a context where land values make up 51 per cent of household wealth, is unlikely to lead to consumer confidence even *without* a deepening cost-of-living crisis. The prospect of a reversal in the ratchet-like system of house prices is not a self-contained problem, but affects the circulation of capital more broadly.

In short, the national economy now works along similar lines to the practice of 'land banking' championed by, among others, property developer Nicholas Barbon in the seventeenth century. 'Old Barbon', as Marx calls him (although his baptismal name, rather splendidly, was If-Jesus-Had-Not-Died-For-Thee-Thou-Wouldst-Be-Damned Barbon), was both emblematic of the early speculative builder-developer and an amateur economist. His writings set out a crude theory of value that merited a number of citations in *Capital*. In the 1690s he set up a land bank, which eventually became a national scheme under the auspices of a 1693 Act of Parliament. The model was that funds would be raised by attracting subscribers who would pledge to invest either cash or titles to land, and the money would then be lent to the government to be repaid with interest. In other words, land was the security for a loan to the government, and subscribers could raise profits through interest payments on the loan.

The wartime government badly needed financing, and it proposed to pay the interest by raising a new tax on salt. The scheme was almost successful: landowners were amazed that they could raise easy money out of nothing more than financial chicanery – pieces of paper raised against their land – and for a moment the National Land Bank even threatened to out-compete the Bank of England and send it to the wall. But there were not enough investors, the national scheme collapsed, and Barbon carried on the bank as a limping private concern until it too collapsed a few years later.[27]

At its height, proponents of such land-banking projects sold them as a panacea: 'There would be no taxes; and yet the Exchequer would be full to overflowing. There would be no poor rates; for there would be no poor. The income of every landowner would be doubled. The profits of every merchant would be increased.' But, as ever, schemes for funding the national economy through property prices came up against hard limits of value. The consensus of the day was that the value of land was no more than twenty years' worth of rental revenue, and that the land bankers had over-valued it in their proposals.[28]

This seventeenth-century approach to land prices is interesting because, like Marx's 'capitalisation' method, it derives the value of land from rental yields. It is a cruder version than Marx's, in that it relies on fixed rents received over an arbitrarily chosen period, rather than the scalable and adjustable method described in *Capital*. But it is notable that there is very august authority for a method of this kind. It is notable, too, that the current economic experiment is not the first time that the government has sought to finance the national economy by a magical system of raising money based on land values.

The Many Victims of the Housing Crisis

Many readers will not have shed tears over the possible collapse described in this chapter. Not only is there a certain poetic justice in landlords and house-price speculators losing a fortune on their investments, especially given the sheer amount of wealth that the renting class has transferred to them, but it might also be thought that a depreciation in accommodation costs is unquestionably a good thing. Unfortunately, though, whether we like it or not, we are all participants in a national economy.

There can be absolutely no doubt that if the mainstay of Britain's wealth fails, the majority of the population – and poorer people especially – will feel the effects. We saw this under the cruel and punitive austerity programme, which was linked to more than 100,000 excess deaths, and caused untold personal hardship, following the global financial crisis. We saw it during the Covid lockdowns, when wealthier peoples' savings and assets grew in value, while so many workers lost wages. Even those of us who enjoy the sheer *schadenfreude* in the prospect of ruined landlords cannot seriously think that they will not take us down with them. If we live in a housing market with an economy attached, our fates are bound together.

In this sense, the sad fact is that 'generation rent' is dependent on its own exploitation. Decades of policy have made society totally dependent on sustaining housing wealth, and it is renters' job to pay for it. A 2016 Resolution Foundation report found that the typical millennial will pay £53,000 in rent before their thirtieth birthday, and their figures are now certain to be out of date.[29] We have put ourselves in a situation in which land value is so fundamental to the economy that, each time these millennial tenants pay half of their income on rent, it is essentially a self-serving act: they are playing their part in ensuring that the national economy does not collapse.

And this is a generation that is used to self-sacrifice. It has suffered the consequences of multiple 'once-in-a-lifetime' economic events. Anyone in their mid thirties will have lived through the 'credit crunch' and ensuing recessions, the consistently falling standards of living (particularly when it comes to housing), the wage stagnation and cuts to services that followed 2008, the Covid-19 pandemic and its economic consequences, and inflation rates that are now seeing records tumble. It would be a great and bitter irony if the one thing that this generation does stand to gain – the much-vaunted massive transfer of wealth through housing inheritance after the rentier generation dies – simply evaporates before it is passed on.

It is worth noting that what we *will not* see if lots of landlords fail is a significant reduction in housing supply. Landlords own homes, but they do not make them. When they sell, they do not knock them down. A reduction in the number of rented homes does not, of course, reduce the number of residential buildings. As the Bank of England's John Lewis and Fergus Cumming explain, writing on the effects of squeezing landlords' profits through taxes and convincingly debunking the myth of 'disappearing landlords',

> *Some* landlords will sell up as letting becomes less lucrative. But at the end of each sales chain is either another landlord or someone who was previously renting. If it's another landlord, aggregate rental supply and demand are both unchanged, and so are rents. If it's a new owner occupier, the supply of rented property has shrunk by one, but so has the number of renters. The tightness of the rental market and thus rents are unchanged.[30]

The whole point about the profitability of the current regime was that it boosted the number of landlords by 2 million, and grew the share of the private rented sector from 7 per cent to 20 per cent. But the death of the landlord industry – the restoration of that 1970s status quo ante – will not lead to a situation with more people than

houses. The homes will still be there. While any market readjustment is going to be painful, it is unlikely that they will stand empty
for ever: landlords will have to sell them to someone, even at rock-
bottom prices, or rent them out if they genuinely cannot.

The winding-down of house prices is something that no government could implement painlessly. It is bound to involve evictions,
repossessions, financial ruin, and human misery as the conflict
between tenants' means and landlords' expectations plays out. The
rot of a rentier economy has set in so deep that it barely seems to
matter who is in power. But what does matter is what we do at the
end of the present housing crisis.

Should we – as governments of the last forty years have done –
desperately try to blow up the housing bubble again, in the hope of
propping up the broader economy? Or should we ensure that we do
not return to a situation where the economy is founded on the
squalid conditions and high costs that working-class renters have to
endure?

There will, of course, be some benefits, and it matters what we
make of them. During similar moments of falling value in the twentieth century, many rented homes were sold to local authorities
with access to preferential public loans. Many homes were also sold
to their sitting tenants or to first-time buyers. Indeed, the term
'gentrification' was first used to describe the phenomenon of aspi-
rational young professionals buying clapped-out homes from
failing landlords in Islington during the era of strict rent controls in
the 1960s. The sheer cost of land has also been a barrier to building
social housing for so long (Shelter and the Local Government
Association have found that the 'high cost of land is the single biggest barrier councils face in getting social housing built'[31]) that
plummeting land values would offer a good opportunity to fix the
problems of previous decades.[32]

An Age of Decadence

A sure sign of a frenzied, crisis-level housing market is a system that has become so valuable that profit-seeking activities burst their former banks, and new channels of profiteering emerge. We saw this in the model of speculative development that came to be sanctioned and regularised in the seventeenth and eighteenth centuries, when speculator-builders came to the fore.

It also emerged in the Victorian period, with the discovery and exploitation of tenurial interests (rather than landownership proper). And we can see it today in the proliferation of parasitic industries like lettings agencies, building and maintenance firms, planning consultants, property lawyers, personal finance and tax advisers, and so on. Everywhere we look, we see signs of the money that trickles down from the housing market.

A 2022 court case, for example, shows how two enterprising east Londoners came across some internet advice about a practice known as the 'rent-to-rent' strategy, and decided – in their own words – to 'get into the property game'. To do this, they needed, they thought, nothing more than an off-the-shelf company, and a landlord who would grant them a perfectly ordinary residential tenancy agreement. They took on a four-bedroom new-build family home in Stratford. They never moved in, but instead sub-let each of the bedrooms and the living room, via the company, to five individual subtenants. Paying tenants were easily found. Indeed, by the time this arrangement came to an end in the summer of 2020, the house was occupied by three individual tenants and a family of five (including three children under the age of six) who had recently moved from Brazil. Collectively, these subtenants paid a higher rent than the original rent on the whole house, and the company was turning an easy profit. Ultimately the head landlord found out, and the subtenants were evicted – but their legal claim for damages against the intermediate landlords was dismissed on a frustrating technical basis.[33] There is plenty of money to be made, particularly by those who operate on the fringes of legality.

Another recent court battle has exposed the troubling trends in the United States at the moment: the gradual privatisation of social housing. This is not taking place along British lines, which saw the mass-scale but highly individual selling off of homes to their residents, but on a more institutional basis. In a typically neoliberal turn of events, capital has realised that social policies – schemes that are intended to achieve the much-needed benefit of ensuring a supply of low-income housing – are backed by state spending, and investors are eager to channel some of the state's generosity towards themselves.

In 2021 the *Financial Times* described how one such scheme worked. In the United States a tax credit programme in effect entitles eligible social housing projects to state funding through a massive reduction in their tax liability. At the end of the 1990s, adopting language typical of the 'Third Way' politics then prevalent in Britain and the United States, charitable housing organisations like New York's RiseBoro entered into a 'partnership' with private equity firms (AIG, in RiseBoro's case). The investors brandished this partnership agreement to the tax authorities, which entitled the *investors* to benefit from the tax credits while allowing working-class homes to be built and maintained using AIG's funding. This involved the transfer of 99.99 per cent of the legal ownership of the homes from the charity to AIG, on the understanding that the homes would then be returned to RiseBoro fifteen years later, when the entitlement to tax credits expired.

When the time came, though, the housing was not given back: AIG betrayed their 'partners', denied that the complex and opaque agreements had ever required the return of ownership, and forced RiseBoro to sue. One of AIG's lawyers is quoted in the press as saying: 'I feel horrible. I will never once again say: "Don't worry,

my client is going to do this, they will walk away after 15 years".'
From my perspective, this is remarkable: the investors are so obviously the bad guys that their own lawyer called them dishonest in a
newspaper. The three-year legal battle was settled in 2022, by
which point AIG's interest had been acquired by our old friends
Blackstone. While RiseBoro regained a majority share of the housing in question, that is a far cry from the investors 'walking away'
and giving the charitable landlord its own homes back.[34]

Until recently, this sort of phenomenon has not been a major
feature of social housing provision in Britain. Traditionally, it has
been local authorities, and more recently housing associations, that
have built social housing. In fact, Britain has sometimes gone to
great lengths to avoid the US-style involvement of big finance in
those projects. For example, in a rather tortuous social-housing
scheme jointly implemented by central government and the Greater
London Authority in 2006, known as the Settled Homes Initiative,
the government funded social landlords to buy back ex-council
homes that had been privatised under the Right to Buy. These
homes would then be rented out to formerly homeless people at
high rents, and the rental profits would help to finance the purchase
of more ex-council homes.

Then, after ten to fifteen years, the tenancies might be 'converted' into affordable social tenancies. Here, instead of funding
coming from private equity, the idea was that low-income tenants
themselves were financing the provision of social housing. Many of
those tenants received Housing Benefit, so this was simply a very
circuitous means of securing the provision of social housing with
funding provided by taxpayers and low-income tenants. Needless
to say, the state was in this case buying back homes it had already
paid for, when local authorities had built them as council housing in
the first place.

This scheme was part of a national programme of convoluted
'products' aimed at tackling the affordable housing shortage

between 2008 and 2011, the weird and wonderful names of which –
New Build HomeBuy, Social HomeBuy, Shared Ownership for the
Elderly, Key Worker Living, Intermediate Rent, Open Market
HomeBuy – illustrate the government's fervent efforts to dig itself
out of a hole by any means except the direct provision of new coun-
cil homes.

But there is a growing trend towards institutional housing
finance in Britain, in both the social and private spheres. In 2021
Lloyds Bank announced its intention of buying 50,000 homes over
four years, which would make it one of the country's biggest landlords. The department store John Lewis is also looking to develop
a corner of the build-to-rent sector by building 10,000 rental units.

If this goes ahead, it would be an almost too perfect symbol of
the institutionalisation of Britain's rental market: the respectable
upper-middle-class corporation replacing the respectable upper-
middle-class individual as the nation's landlord. While Britain is
still overwhelmingly dominated by small-business-owner landlords, the direct rule of large-scale capital in the rental market
appears to be on the rise.

Socialism or Barbonism

Britain is not immune from the US-style mélange of housing
finance and social landlordism. A great deal of the new social housing being built is wrenched from private developers as a condition
for the grant of planning permission. But capital is also finding ever
more sophisticated ways of using well-intentioned social housing
projects for its own gain.

As the housing crisis has dragged on, we have seen the erosion of
the traditional 'municipal socialism' model of public housing provision, under which councils would directly build homes for social
rent, and its replacement with a system of state-sponsored for-profit
development with crumbs of affordable housing. Just as the early

property developers made profitable use of aristocrats' manorial estates, private capital is finding increasingly sophisticated ways to make money from public land.

At the more outrageous and unashamed end of the scale is Manchester Life – a joint venture between Manchester City Council and the Abu Dhabi United Group. A report by academics at the University of Sheffield has shown just how profoundly the city council has been shaken down by Abu Dhabi development capital.[35] Swathes of urban public land were sold at undervalued prices on 999-year leases. Unusually for Britain, this is a large-scale project of build-to-rent corporate landlordism, with the rents on the new developments going to Abu Dhabi alone rather than to the joint venture, so that Manchester Council does not even benefit from the rental income. There are no social housing obligations attached to the project.

Astonishingly, the city even contributes to the financing of this redevelopment using public money loans. The financial benefits to the council are unclear at best, and the University of Sheffield report is pessimistic about them. And the eighteenth-century landowners at least got their land back when the development leases expired – but who knows whether Manchester will even exist in the year 3,000? In the meantime, capital is going to do exceedingly well out of the city's residents.

Other councils have been wooed into more complicated commitments by the latter-day Nicholas Barbons. The London Borough of Havering, for example, is one of many councils that has been hamstrung for decades by legal restrictions on the use of its housing revenue account. Put simply, the HRA is a ring-fenced fund into which council tenants pay their rent, and there are strict limits on how it can be used, making it very difficult for councils to use this money to finance new building projects of their own.

But there is increasing excitement on the housing-finance scene about 'unlocking' HRAs by performing a variety of new tricks. In

2018 Havering entered into a joint venture with private house-builder Wates to carry out a large-scale redevelopment of its estates, involving a significant amount of market-rate homes being built for private sale. The sophistication here is that the council is partly funding the redevelopment through its HRA, on the basis that at least some of the new homes will be social housing. To put it another way: the council has found a way of using its own ring-fenced funds to sponsor someone else's profitable redevelopment project, so that private capital does not have to perform its traditional role of stumping up all of the funding. For Wates, the project represents a £1 billion contract.[36] It is difficult to imagine the aristocratic landowners of previous centuries making such fools of themselves by paying for someone else's development project – particularly in such an overwhelmingly profitable environment.

What the Havering model shows is that capital does not need to own the freehold to turn a profit from housing: the council is keeping the land, but Wates is profiting from the building and sales prices. This is why projects that examine landownership alone, like Guy Shrubsole's *Who Owns England?*, can miss the point. Ownership is not everything. Even Brett Christophers's more sophisticated and persuasive argument against privatisation logic in *The New Enclosures* calls for some refinement: development profiteering can take place even where land has not been privatised at all, but remains fully publicly owned.

This is often the case when it comes to 'property guardianship' schemes, many of which concern state-owned buildings like schools, care homes and NHS facilities. The guardianship companies tend to own no legal interest in the land whatsoever; they do not even hold a tenancy. They generally own – or even just belong to a group of companies *one of which* owns – a mere contractual right over the land (known legally as a personal licence). But because that licence gives them effective control of the land, they can make an enormous amount of profit.

In a recent legal case I was involved in, which concerned a disused clinic owned by the NHS, the guardianship company was charging ten occupiers about £400 each per month. The guardianship company was thus making £4,000 per month from a piece of public land essentially without costs, because the guardians themselves were paying to look after the building. Nothing was privatised or sold off; nothing changed hands.

The closer we approach to a collapse, the more we come to realise that risk is for the little people (petty landlords and homeowners) and for local authorities. Big capital prefers to borrow land, or to build and sell new homes, rather than expose itself to the longer-term risks involved in ownership and letting. The model they use here is often tenurial: it is more reminiscent of Georgian building leases, or the 'rent-to-rent' strategy described above, or the Victorian mania for trading sub-interests, than of the corporate buyouts seen in the United States, Spain and Germany. The housing crisis in Britain is more nuanced than elsewhere.

With the successes of this model, rent-seeking has surely entered a dangerous, decadent phase. Empty public buildings are generating free money for private companies. Councils' ring-fenced public money is being channelled into developers' hands. House builders, developers and equity providers can turn excellent profits while signally failing to solve the housing crisis. To mix a metaphor: local authorities are getting in on the top floor, while capital itself is well-placed to disappear when the music stops. It plays only a fleeting role. We are left to wonder what it is afraid of. What can it see on the horizon?

The Impossible Dream

The real estate services firm Savills works with a great many local authorities, providing advice and expertise on housing and finance. One of the wares Savills is currently flogging is the 'East London

Corridor Development': a concept that spans seven local authority areas. The area is, says Savills, 'the most affordable area of London'. So what does Savills want to do with it? Make it unaffordable, of course.[37] 'There is a clear need', says Savills, 'to ramp up housing delivery across the capital, but none more so than in London's eastern corridor.' The plan is to build thousands of new homes, capitalising in particular on government schemes such as Shared Ownership and First Homes, which give the illusion of transforming expensive new homes into affordable ones. In reality, of course, the regeneration model of building market-rate new homes with a small number of government-scheme homes as a bolt-on tends to raise local prices and eliminate affordability.

Thus, the ultimate aim – or at least likely outcome – is to tear apart one of the only parts of the capital in which poorer people can currently afford to live; and this model is being pursued all over the country. Assuming for a moment that these gentrifying schemes work as intended, rather than collapsing, what happens when there is nowhere left that is affordable to lower-income households? By general agreement, low-income households are essential for capitalism to function, so this is a moment of crisis. The contradictions of capitalism are asserting themselves. The housing crisis is not sustainable, and we cannot regenerate our way out of it.

This is a problem because local authorities themselves are increasingly 'getting into the property game'. For example, Brent, a London borough with significant levels of deprivation, is the sole owner of a corporate private landlord called I4B. The idea is that its profits – being the council's profits – will fund much-needed social housing in the borough. Similar ideas are seen increasingly often these days – especially in south-east England: Homes for Lambeth, Croydon's Brick by Brick, the Haringey Development Vehicle, and many others.

This system works on roughly the same logic as a perpetual-motion machine. Profits from the housing crisis will fuel the solutions to the housing crisis. Extracting market-level rents from the working class will alleviate poverty in the borough. It is madness to think that a significant institutional landlord, or any entity that bases its business model on speculating on ground rents, will not simply make matters worse. Owen Hatherley makes a compelling argument that, when it comes to property development, councils should take the same approach recommended in relation to fossil fuels, and 'leave it in the ground'.[38] And if we are trading slogans with other campaigns, I would urge councils to take the same approach to residential buildings as the Dogs Trust takes with pets, and never destroy a healthy one.

The profound effects of a reversal in the housing crisis were discussed earlier in this chapter. But councils that have been banking on redevelopment are especially vulnerable to a housing downturn. Croydon Council's scheme – Brick by Brick – brought the council to its knees even while house prices were still rising. Lambeth Council's flagship scheme was condemned in a high-profile review by a retired senior civil servant.[39] The councillors who pursued these schemes so fervently will have a lot to answer for when the downturn comes.

The most remarkable thing about housing in Britain is its insufferable continuous growth. What goes up stubbornly refuses to come down. It is therefore incredibly dangerous to make predictions about a house-price crash: everyone who has done so for the last twenty-five years has been proved wrong. But there are genuine reasons to doubt that it can survive the current economic circumstances. While it is impossible to say anything for certain, what does seem clear is that *if* the housing market survives, it will be because something new and unexpected has happened – like the effects of quantitative easing in 2009. Capital is resilient, and none more so than British real estate; but it is surely laughable to suppose that the present circumstances – in which every single morning we wake up to find that the value of the national housing stock has increased by £750 million since the day before – are going to last for ever.

Conclusion:
A World without Landlords

*It seems that a law directed at such injustice and greed has never been
drafted in such restrained and generous terms: it ordered those men (who
should have been punished for their transgressions, fined, and required to
give back the lands) merely to walk away from the lands which they had
unjustly obtained, accepting the full price for it, and providing it to their
fellow citizens who were in need of assistance.*

Plutarch's 'Life of Tiberius Gracchus'

The housing crisis is a tale of conflict. The system of housing
wealth in Britain is characterised by conflict between renters and
owners, conflict between generations, between regions, between
racial groups. The simple fact that underpins the bitterness we feel
about our housing situation is that, in each case, the more disadvantaged of each of those groups is transferring wealth to the
better-off. Renters prop up house prices, as each month they justify
the speculative value of housing assets by paying an ever-increasing
amount to rentiers. Whiter, older people in wealthier areas benefit
at the cost of everyone else.

Marx was at pains to point out that virtually everyone's economic interests are aligned against those of landlords. Tenants'
interests obviously are, but employers, too, have tended to prefer
lower rents (and a consequently lower wage bill). Historically,

states have leaned against excessive land speculation and preferred to focus their policies on profitable industries, even where this comes at the price of diminishing landlords' economic power. But the key to understanding our housing crisis is the realisation that housing assets are now at the core of the national economy. Because house prices are founded on ever-rising rents, landlords' interests and homeowners' interests have become elided. And because homeownership and housing wealth are so important to Britain's post-industrial economy, renters' interests are in conflict with the national interest.

In moments of economic flux, the state now routinely tries to stimulate the property market at the expense of the renting population. In 2022 the *New Statesman* published data showing that the Housing Benefit bill was so high that only three government departments – Health and Social Care, Education, and Defence – have budgets that are bigger than this single item of the Department for Work and Pensions' spending.[1]

But even that £23.4 billion annual bill does not come close to alleviating poverty or hardship. On the contrary: every time the government lowers stamp duty or underwrites mortgages or funds developers to gentrify working-class districts, it drives up housing costs. These costs, of course, are merely passed on to tenants and the state itself, due to the legal environment of unchecked rents. The City of London – which traditionally intervenes when social spending rises too high for its liking – has been curiously untroubled by these wasted billions.

But the legal framework upon which house-price capitalism was built has now become too successful for its own good. Homes are so valuable that ownership rates are declining. Rents and housing costs are prohibitive for local working populations, and the contradictions of capitalism are on full display. Labour mobility – one of the original aims underlying insecure housing[2] – has been replaced with labour precarity, and with wage bills that are putting an unmanageable strain on employers. For the time being, though, government policy still seems to be aimed at squeezing as much wealth as possible out of housing, rather than undermining or changing the conditions that make it so profitable in the first place.

This book has sought to draw together the strands of law, policy and economics that have conspired to create these conditions: to give an account of how the abolition of rent controls fed into a situation in which councils have to treat living rooms as bedrooms when they come to accommodate people, and persistently fail to procure dwellings that meet even those miserable standards. Poor housing law leads directly to housing crisis. The crisis has now reached a point where there will need to be political responses, and the central question is what our aims and methods should be.

Homes under the Hammer (and Sickle)

Thankfully, a consensus has grown in recent years around the need to expand the stock of council housing. For some readers, this might seem like a timid and rather statist position, but there are two responses to that concern. The first is that this is a book about capitalism – and, more precisely, about housing under capitalism. Rejecting Engels's argument that nothing can be done about the housing question unless private property itself is abolished, we can make great strides towards alleviating the sort of housing misery that we see today, even assuming that capitalism endures. We can reduce the intensity of our exploitation and housing stress. Accommodating people more cheaply, securely and under good conditions is by far the best method of achieving that.

Second, pursuing a massive increase in council housing may not, after all, be such a moderate policy, because it chimes with some of the earliest thinking around communism. Marx and Engels's 1848 *Communist Manifesto* calls not for the complete abolition of rent, but for rents to be paid as a form of taxation – which is effectively what council rents are. The first demand of the *Manifesto* is for the 'abolition of property in land and *application of all rents of land to public purposes*'.[3] Council tenants pay their rents to the local authority, and the money can only be spent on the 'public purpose' of funding and maintaining the council housing itself.

While council housing rents are not exactly the sort of general taxation that Marx and Engels had in mind, mass social housing would mean more rents going towards public purposes rather than private landowners. In the last century, council housing began to knock some of the roughest edges off the capitalist mode of production. This is the remarkable thing about the mid-twentieth-century consensus around large-scale public housing, and the Tories' impressive record in building it: there was a time when, to an extent, even arch-Thatcherites like Keith Joseph made common cause with the communists.

In an 1872 speech in Manchester to the International Workingmen's Association, Marx argued that 'the social movement will lead to this decision that the land can but be owned by the nation itself'.[4] A century later, the growth of the social state caused journalist Simon Jenkins to write: 'It may well be that the days of private land ownership, at least in the central areas of a city like London, are over.' But all of that progress was undone. We dismantled the council housing system, and replaced it with one in which £88 billion is paid to residential landlords every year.

This is the point about a mass council housing project: it does not benefit the tenants alone, but interferes significantly in the political economy of land. Even within a capitalist system, it 'makes possible a rational and democratic system in which the allocation of housing services and housing costs is no longer left to the hidden, grasping hand of the market'.[5] And beyond that, if Jenkins is to be believed, the twentieth-century social state was so staggeringly successful that it threatened the nature of private landownership itself. With this in mind, James Connolly's famous remark, 'For our demands most moderate are, we only want the earth', begins to lose its sense of contradiction.

In the 1980s, the state deliberately halted the terminal decline of the private landlord. It was within our grasp, and we reversed it. When we talk about abolishing landlordism, it is not pie-in-the-sky. In fact it is probably more immediately achievable than, say, police or prison abolition. As far back as 1965, the Milner Holland committee felt the need to advise the Douglas-Home government: 'We do not think that the role of private landlords is finished.'[6] Both the left and the right then spent the next fifteen years becoming increasingly convinced that the writing was on the wall for privately rented homes; today, we need landlords to regain that sense of peril if we are to fix this crisis. For the time being, however, the divine right of landlords is so deeply entrenched that there is a media panic whenever a political party moots introducing pet-friendly policies for tenants.

During the Victorian experiment in '5 per cent philanthropy', there was a complaint among the 'ethical' investors that the better social landlords (notably Peabody Trust) were undercutting the competition, thereby rendering the 5 per cent investment schemes unprofitable. The secretary of the Metropolitan Association was anxious that Peabody was 'at least 30 per cent under the market, and they are working a serious injury against us'.[7] This is precisely the point. Large-scale, non-profit-seeking models of housing provision are capable of driving rent-seekers out of business, and that must be our aim.

This may be the perfect moment for revisiting municipalisation. As we saw in Chapter 2, a collapse in housing values both after the Second World War and again in the 1970s meant that public authorities were primed to take over ownership of land and housing. Where preferential loans and public grants are available, and falling values mean that landlords are keen to sell, conditions are perfect for replenishing social housing stocks in the form of existing buildings. And housing, of course, tends to pay for itself in the longer term.

The only concern is that new-build construction standards in Britain are so notoriously bad that local authorities may end up with expensive, and possibly dangerous, privately built stock. But rebuilding council housing as a move towards the decommodification of housing must be at the heart of our project. The worst thing we could do after any house-price crash would be to wind the housing crisis back up again.

Things We Used to Know

The problem faced by opponents of rent controls is that their main public-relations tactic is the scare story. They borrow disasters from other times and places, and attempt to make us worry about 'shadow markets' or 'disappearing landlords'. But in the context of such a severe housing crisis, these counterfactuals sound like something of a relief. It would be very difficult for the landlord lobby to come up with a situation that is much worse than what we have today.

Rent controls are more than just a weak compromise with the landlord class, a staging post on the route to a better society. When they work, just like large-scale council housing, they create the conditions for reducing or eliminating the exploitative private rented sector. Again, the experience of the 1970s shows us how rent controls can work to partially decommodify housing markets to great effect. It was only fifty years ago that political parties and activists were making serious plans for a post-landlord society, and we should welcome any step that brings us closer to that situation.

This is what is so frustrating about so much of the housing policy debate over the last few years. Today's accounts of the housing crisis are invariably based on neoclassical economics. This has led to elaborate debates about the precise effects of housing supply, a confected conflict between NIMBYs and YIMBYs, and a universal acceptance that there is a housing shortage. And – while everyone acknowledges that things are very bad, and that there is a need for drastic intervention of some kind – political parties wring their hands and claim that pandering to property developers is the only viable solution. This displays a complete ignorance of the history of housing and land policy. It shows that we have forgotten about the price controls that dominated housing policy throughout the twentieth century, and that their strategies were far more successful than our own. We used to know about the ways in which laws had an effect on land and housing provision; it now seems as if we have even forgotten how to talk about these ideas.

Consider, for example, the 100 per cent development charge mentioned in Chapter 1. This, like the licence requirement that stumped Gabriel Harrison, was specifically designed to dampen a frenzy of post-war commercial property speculation, and it was very effective. 'Land values are being, by this Bill, substantially deflated', boasted Hugh Dalton, Attlee's chancellor of the exchequer; 'this source of land speculation will be stopped for ever'. Dalton claimed, over-ambitiously: 'we are moving towards the nationalisation of the land, and not by slow steps'. Indeed, he described the measure in parliament as being 'the workers' revenge for the enclosures'.[8]

Imagine how a serious government could put such a dampening measure into force today. A simple, radical tax measure could bring an instant halt to a system predicated on price speculation. If there were a 100 per cent capital gains tax, it would be in no one's interest for house prices to go up. If we wanted to, we could end house-price speculation instantly, as the tenants' revenge for the immense wealth that the housing crisis has prised from them.

Realistically, though, reform is unlikely to be as dramatic or sharp as that; but there is cause for optimism. Years before I started writing this book, no-fault evictions had been something of a hobby-horse of mine, and I had been trying hard to persuade people of the economic consequences of unstable tenancies. But there was no appetite for reform in England. National housing charities seemed to treat a campaign for private-sector security as politically naive, and even a Corbyn-led Labour Party started out by recycling Cameron- and Miliband-era pledges of short 'family friendly' tenancies.

A 2018 opposition Green Paper, *Housing for the Many*, contained some fairly tired material focusing on the social sector. Some colleagues and I drafted a response on behalf of the Society of Labour Lawyers explaining the need for the abolition of section 21, and in late 2018 it felt like a demand that was outrageous and obscure in equal measure. But – to our amazement – the Labour front bench suddenly committed to the policy a few months later, in March 2019. While we will never know whether anyone at the Labour Party had even read our pitch, what is certain is that each of the other major political parties felt the need to match Labour's pledge at that year's general election, and we went into the 2019 parliament with an unimpeachable political consensus in favour of dismantling a key element of Thatcherism. The effects of that change are likely to be felt in the medium and long term rather than immediately. But we may be heading towards the sort of legal framework that was in place before the present housing crisis started to take shape.

Many of the proposals for housing reform that are advanced today focus on tax reform. Commentators see the vast wealth that housing generates, and consider it to be an important, radical measure to capture some of that wealth and deploy it for socially useful purposes. But these methods can be quite difficult to put into effect. Despite the enthusiastic efforts of movements like the Georgists in the nineteenth and twentieth centuries, tax advocates routinely come to find that land is only easily taxable at the point of sale – which happens rarely – and that efforts to impose ongoing land taxation require both a sophisticated apparatus for valuing land and liquidity on the part of the landowner, which is not always feasible when land has quickly appreciated in value.

But, more fundamentally, there is something of a tension between measures that aim to capture landed wealth and policies that seek to undermine its value in the first place. We can be intensely relaxed about house-price growth as long as the speculators pay their taxes; or we can take the Hugh Dalton line of using the law to deflate property values. The latter aims to solve the housing crisis, while the former seeks merely to offset some of its effects. There seems to be little point in maintaining a situation in which people face very high housing costs but some of the money is recouped by the state, when we could aim instead to lower those housing costs drastically in the first place.

Bastard Landlords

A few years ago, a friend of mine was looking after a cat as part of a scheme that fosters pets belonging to families who are temporarily homeless as a result of fleeing domestic violence. My friend had a week's holiday booked, and asked if the cat could stay in my shared flat. I made the mistake of running it past our letting agent, who refused outright. There was an increasingly bitter exchange of emails in which I asked whether they had even bothered to ask the landlord (they had not, but it was policy). I tend to pride myself on maintaining my cool, lawyerly demeanour in almost all of my dealings, but a red mist began to descend. Shane McGowan's lyrics from 'The Bastard Landlord' echoed around my head and raised my blood pressure. I ended up sending some replies that I am now too ashamed to recall.

Leaving aside for a moment the more direct harm of evictions, rent increases and tenancy churn, landlords and their agents have an extraordinary degree of day-to-day control over society: 2.5

million totally unremarkable people dictate the behaviour of 4.4 million households. Can I have a pet? Can I hang a picture? Can I replace the lumpy 'landlord special' mattress on the 'landlord special' double divan, on which I am required to sleep every night? Our thoughts turn to the deposit whenever something happens to the physical space, and we spend thousands on utility bills rather than bothering our exploiters with complaints about leaking pipes and ancient boilers.

Renting in Britain is so deeply infantilising that – where it does not build resentment and rage – it is bound to feed into a sense of individual inferiority towards the landlord or their twenty-year-old property manager. We have, I suspect, also seen the de-skilling of a generation, as millions of people have no experience of carrying out works on their own homes. And we are paying well over the odds, in international or historical terms, for the privilege.

Building the Future

Engels's argument that there is always a housing crisis under capitalism was predicated on the idea of constant and acute housing shortage. But that is not the crisis we face. We are the heirs to record-breaking amounts of municipal construction (much of which still physically exists), and to an economy built upon property development. The vast majority of homes in England and Wales – about 70 per cent – are underoccupied. Scarcity of buildings is not the problem. We have a relative abundance, in historical or geographically comparative terms, but a crisis of price. And crisis, as explained in the previous chapter, tends to reach a point at which it needs to resolve itself. House-price capitalism may finally begin to enter a phase of decline.

What has struck me most while writing this book is how Marx's point about urban rents being, in effect, monopoly prices has been proved right over and over again. It seems astonishing that the point is not made more often. We have seen examples from Victorian Britain, from fin de siècle Naples, from colonial Mumbai, from Hong Kong, and elsewhere: throughout modern history, unregulated land markets have led to deteriorating conditions and soaring rents, even where wages have stagnated or fallen. To those I would add probably the most pertinent example from a contemporary British perspective: 1990s Cairo. In that decade, a land boom overtook both tourism and manufacturing, making it Egypt's third-largest non-oil investment sector, and vast amounts of housing were built. But the glut of new buildings only made the housing crisis worse. Squalor intensified, and lower-waged workers were pushed into a distant peri-urban sprawl. 'Upwards of a million apartments stand empty', wrote a contemporary observer. 'There is no housing shortage per se. In fact, Cairo is filled with buildings that are half-empty.'[9]

The simple fact is that, where rents are unrestrained by law, they can reach monopoly prices – and those monopoly prices determine land values. Building more housing is an article of faith, but there is little point in increasing supply if the legal and economic conditions will always allow the grasping hand of the market to feel around for the limits of people's means.

This book is about housing – but housing is, of course, one of many interconnected issues. The housing crisis – the need to maintain housing value and extract wealth – rests upon inadequate systems of pensions, wages and public services. A common interest is shared between those who intend to retire and the maintainers of the housing crisis, so it is difficult to unpick the relationship between the two. But, on the other side of the equation, a common interest is also shared between housing crisis opponents and other groups. The class of homeowners is shrinking, and the needs of renters and homeless people are becoming more urgent than demands for pensions. But, perhaps more importantly, there is a growing convergence between housing and environmental concerns.

When future generations come to study the beginnings of the end of the world, even the most unobservant and ideologically minded will have to concede that its causes began with capitalism. A system predicated on private accumulation, and wilfully blind to social need, is at the heart of climate breakdown. Nowhere is this more obvious than in the built environment.

On a routine basis, we see the ritual tearing-down of viable buildings for redevelopment. Large publicly built estates like Central Hill in south London are being demolished before our eyes, then rebuilt for sale at a higher price – raising costs for everyone locally, and driving poorer people away; and even based on the local authority's case, the net gain in the number of homes is slim. This is a gross act of ecological vandalism and social violence, masquerading as a solution to the housing crisis. There is an ever more pressing case for winding down house-price capitalism on ecological grounds, as we continue to exceed our planetary boundaries.

With each passing year, the growing generation of renters has less to lose. By definition, it has no assets. Its rented homes are not particularly worth fighting for. The pace of planetary destruction increases. The forces that drive its political commitment are becoming ever more powerful. Both Black Lives Matter and the Stansted 15 protesters took direct action to block runways because they wanted to draw attention to the intertwined nature of climate breakdown, colonialism, deportations and fossil fuels. In a similar way, the housing movement would do well to combine its energies with climate and anti-racism activists to ensure that property development loses its central role in the debate over the housing crisis. We must draw attention to its inherent racism and its ecological destructiveness, as well as its impoverishing effects.

The system of house-price growth was not designed to be wound down gently or peacefully. As a country, we have bet the farm on house prices, and successive governments have been understandably cautious about altering the laws designed to encourage homes to become more expensive. But the scale of the harm of this system can no longer be denied. We owe it to ourselves to change things. We owe it, in particular, to the deceased and survivors of Grenfell. We owe it also to people like Daniel Gauntlett, a homeless man who died of cold outside a boarded-up bungalow a few months after squatting was criminalised, sacrificed to a temporary moral panic about property values; to Mizanur Rahman, who died from a fire in an East End slum in 2023, within a mile of a major world financial centre; to Awaab Ishak, who died, aged two, after his social landlord blamed his parents for the dangerous mould in their rented home; and to the homeless people dying at a rate of one every six-and-a-half hours. We owe it to the countless people who have suffered psychological and physical harm or distress as a result of housing instability, or were driven away from their homes and communities by ever-increasing costs.

By methods as prosaic as law reform, we can work towards decommodifying housing, and drive landlords and house-price speculators from the face of the earth. We have done it before, and we must do it again.

Acknowledgements

Leo Hollis and the Verso team very bravely took on a first-time author, whose two main prose influences were *Das Kapital* and the law reports, and somehow managed to coax this book into becoming something readable. It has been a pleasure to work with such a skilful and enthusiastic publishing house.

I owe huge thanks to my family. To my parents, Andrew and Elizabeth, to Chris, Madeline, Tim and Felicity, and – most especially – to Harry and Amélie, who bring us all so much joy.

For several years I have been reading Marx and associated texts as part of a reading group. I am sure they would prefer me not to name them individually, so I will simply say that their generosity and their knowledge are just extraordinary. Without them I would have had such a fundamentally different understanding of the world, and each one of them has enriched both my thinking and my life in general. I hope that the analysis in this book is a credit to them.

There were some rare friends whom I trusted enough to send drafts for comment. They not only improved the content enormously, but skilfully managed to keep my ego intact. Love and thanks to Alva Gotby, David Renton, Eamon Rooke, Gargi Bhattacharyya, Jack McGinn, Kasia Tomasiewicz, Laurène Veale and Michael Engelhardt-Sprack.

I'm very grateful to Owen Hatherley, who was characteristically generous in helping me to get this project off the ground. He had also encouraged a good deal of my earlier writing on this subject, and you will see the influence of his own work throughout this book. Similarly, many of the ideas here began as discussions among a small and inventive group of housing thinkers, including Isaac Rose, Lily Gordon Brown, Joe Bilsborough, Siobhan Donnachie and Sarah Doyle. We came together as a self-organised group of strangers, linked only by a shared interest, but this turned out to be an excellent way of doing things and I would recommend it to anyone.

I have leaned very heavily on my friends, and I would particularly like to thank Margherita Philipp, Daniel Nicol, Domhnall McFarline, Angharad Monk, Popi Wilson, Pip Tomes, Margaux Joly, Hannah Webb, Jaemie, Paolo Farina, Seema Syeeda, Sabrina Huck and Dan Frost. I owe so many of the book's ideas to conversations with friends, and the arguments here have been shaped in no small part by Deivi Norberg, Franck Magennis, Roya Sarrafi-Gohar, Zehrah Hasan, Kane Shaw, Gabriela Salva Macallan, Nathaniel Mckenzie, josie sparrow and Tom Gann.

I would also like to thank my formidable colleagues in the housing team at Garden Court Chambers (corralled by my friend and teacher Liz Davies) and its clerking team (led by the excellent Tim Hempstead). It was only because I had their support and their professional solidarity that I could make the space to write this book.

Finally, to my comrades in the housing movement, whether we know each other personally or not. Readers will have seen how much of this book has come about due to my involvement in Housing Action Southwark and Lambeth. My early days of organising with them – particularly with Izzy, Luke, Chloë, Jaemie, Fowsiyo, Joe, and many others – was a deeply formative experience for me, and I greatly appreciate them all. More recently it has been a privilege to be in closer contact with Greater Manchester Housing Action and London Renters Union. This book is for the people in the struggle for better housing and a better world.

Notes

Introduction: House-Price Capitalism

1. OECD Affordable Housing Database, Figs HM1.1 and PH4.2.1, at oecd.org.
2. Rupert Jones, 'Private Rents in Britain Hit Record Highs, with 20% Rise in Some Areas', *Guardian*, 21 October 2022.
3. OECD Affordable Housing Database, Fig. HC3.1. While this figure (unlike other states' data) includes households that are 'threatened with homelessness', this very concept is a necessary consequence of the UK's extraordinarily insecure system of private tenancies, which puts renters at constant risk of eviction, so it is probably a fair comparison.
4. Wendy Wilson and Cassie Barton, *Households in Temporary Accommodation (England)*, House of Commons Library, 30 January 2023, p. 11.
5. National Housing Federation, *Briefing: Overcrowding in England* (April 2023), p. 6.
6. Vicky Spratt, 'Women Face Growing Gender Housing Gap as Rents, House Prices and Wage Inequality Spiral', *i News*, 15 March 2022, at inews.co.uk.
7. Museum of Homelessness, *Findings: Dying Homeless Project*, 17 September 2022, at museumofhomelessness.org.
8. Arj Singh, 'Rise in Rough Sleeping Prompts Warnings Tories Could Break Election Manifesto Pledge on Homelessness', *i News*, 30 December 2022, at inews.co.uk.
9. Resolution Foundation, *Housing Outlook Q3 2022*, 17 September 2022, at resolutionfoundation.org.
10. Ibid.
11. Jim Connolly and James Stewart, 'Private Renters Stuck in Dangerous Homes "Failed" by Councils', BBC News, 10 November 2022, at bbc.co.uk.
12. Office for National Statistics, *Housing, England and Wales: Census 2021* (statistical bulletin), 5 January 2023.

13. Anthony Breach, 'Population growth isn't causing the housing shortage – the planning system is', *Conservative Home*, 17 June 2023, at conservativehome.com.

14. Sophus zu Ermgassen, Michal Dreniok, Joseph W. Bull, Christine Corlet Walker, Mattia Mancini, Josh Ryan-Collins and André Cabrera Serrenho, 'A Home for All within Planetary Boundaries, Pathways for Meeting England's Housing Needs without Transgressing National Climate and Biodiversity Goals', OSF Preprints, 8 March 2022, doi:10.1016/j.ecolecon.2022.107562.

1. The Ratchet System

1. Oliver Marriott, *The Property Boom* (London: Hamish Hamilton, 1967), p. 11.

2. Greg Pitcher, 'Foster + Partners' Mayfair Luxury Hotel Approved', *Architects' Journal*, 3 July 2019.

3. Town and Country Planning Act 1947, Part VII.

4. Marriott, *The Property Boom*, p. 22.

5. Historic England, *The Late 20th-Century Commercial Office: Introductions to Heritage Assets* (London: Historic England, 2016).

6. Manfredo Tafuri, *The Sphere and the Labyrinth* (Cambridge, MA: MIT, 1990). For an application of this principle to London, see Owen Hatherley, *A Guide to the New Ruins of Great Britain* (London: Verso, 2011), pp. 342–3.

7. Valeria Ricciuli, 'Brooklyn NYCHA Complex to Sell Air Rights in First-of-Its-Kind Deal', *Curbed*, 11 October 2019, at ny.curbed.com.

8. Brett Christophers, 'Mind the Rent Gap: Blackstone, Housing Investment and the Reordering of Urban Rent Surfaces', *Urban Studies* 59: 4 (11 August 2021); Blackstone Property Holdings Partners Europe Holdings S.à r.l., *2019 Annual Report*, p. 48.

9. *Hansard*, House of Commons, 8 July 1963 (HC Debs vol. 680 col. 872).

10. Wendy Wilson, *A Short History of Rent Control*, House of Commons Library, 30 March 2017, p. 9.

11. Anna Minton, *Big Capital: Who Is London For?* (London: Penguin, 2017), p. 53.

12. Built Environment Committee, House of Lords, *Meeting Housing Demand*, 10 January 2022, p. 5.

13. Ministry of Housing, Communities and Local Government, *English Housing Survey: Headline Report, 2019–20*, p. 33.

14. Leslie Kern, *Gentrification Is Inevitable and Other Lies* (London: Verso, 2023), p. 52.

15. Office for National Statistics, *Housing Affordability in England and Wales: 2021* (statistical bulletin), 23 March 2022, p. 4 – at ons.gov.uk.

16. Christophers, 'Mind the Rent Gap'. Emphasis in original.

17. Phillipe Askenazy, *Share The Wealth: How to End Rentier Capitalism* (London: Verso, 2021), p. 55.

18. *Rent Act 1957 (Inquiry Report)* – *Hansard*, p. 25.

19. Adam Smith, *An Inquiry into the Nature and Causes of the Wealth of Nations*, cited in Karl Marx, 'Rent of Land', *Economic and Philosophic Manuscripts of 1844*, available at marxists.org; Karl Marx, *Theories of Surplus Value*, 1863, volume II, chapter VIII 3(b) ('Formulation of the Problem of Rent') and 3(c) ('Private Ownership of the Land as a Necessary Condition for the Existence of Absolute Rent. Surplus-Value in Agriculture Resolves into Profit and Rent').

20. John Burnett, *A Social History of Housing 1815–1970* (Exeter: David & Charles, 1978), p. 215.

21. *Morning Chronicle*, 16 September 1850 – cited in Burnett, *Social History of Housing*, p. 41.

22. Minton, *Big Capital*, pp. 85–5.

23. Trust for London, 'Rent for a One Bedroom Dwelling as a Percentage of Gross Pay by London Borough (April 2021 to March 2022)', *London's Poverty Profile*, at trustforlondon.org.uk.

24. Sam Ray-Chaudhuri and Tom Waters, 'Freezes in Housing Support Widen Geographic Disparities for Low-Income Renters', Institute for Fiscal Studies, 3 February 2023 – at ifs.org.uk.

25. Hamptons Estate Agents, 'Annual Rent Bill to hit £63bn', July 2022, at hamptons.co.uk; Afiq Fitri, 'The UK Now Spends More on Housing Benefit than on Most Government Departments', *New Stateman*, 14 November 2022.

26. Marx, 'Rent of Land'.

27. David Harvey, *The Limits to Capital* (London: Verso, 2018), p. 371.

28. See, for example, *Banking on Property: What Is Driving the Housing Crisis and How to Solve It*, Positive Money, March 2022, at trustforlondon.org.uk.

29. A. W. B Simpson, *An Introduction to the History of Land Law* (Oxford: OUP, 1961), p. 6.

30. Karl Marx, *Capital: Volume III* (London: Penguin, 1991), p. 944.

31. Harvey, *Limits to Capital*, p. 347.

32. Ibid., p. 368.

33. This is explored in more detail in Chapter 2.

34. See, for example, Sam Bright, *Fortress London: Why We Need to Save the Country from Its Capital* (Manchester: Harper North, 2022), p. 88.

35. Hamptons, 'Annual Rent Bill to Hit £63bn'.

36. Quoted in Stuart Hodkinson, *Safe as Houses: Private Greed, Political Negligenge and Housing Policy after Grenfell* (Manchester: Manchester University Press, 2019), p. 61.

2. A Longer View

1. Proclamation of 1580, cited in Norman G. Brett-James, *The Growth of Stuart London* (London: London & Middlesex Archaeological Society, 1935), p. 69; Erection of Cottages Act 1588.

2. Repertories of the Court of Aldermen – cited in Brett-James, *Growth of Stuart London*, Chapter 3.

3. W. Edward Riley and George Laurence Gomme, eds, 'Lincoln's Inn Fields: Introduction', in *Survey of London: Volume 3, St Giles-in-the-Fields, Pt. I: Lincoln's Inn Fields* (1912), available at british-history.ac.uk.

4. Eric Hobsbawm, *The Age of Empire* (London: Weidenfeld & Nicolson, 1987), p. 343 – cited in Ellen Meiksins Wood, *The Origins of Capitalism: A Longer View* (London: Verso, 2002), Chapter 6, footnote 3.

5. E. P. Thompson, *The Making of the English Working Class* (London: Penguin, 1991), p. 355.

6. Henry-Russell Hitchcock, *Early Victorian Architecture in Britain*, vol. I, (London: Architectural Press, 1954), p. 409.

7. Gareth Stedman Jones, *Outcast London: A Study in the Relationship Between Classes in Victorian Society* (London: Verso, 2013), p. 209.

8. Avner Offer, *Property and Politics 1870–1914: Landownership, Law, Ideology and Urban Development in England* (Cambridge: CUP, 1981), pp. 102–3.

9. Offer, *Property and Politics*, p. 119.

10. Ibid., p. 123.

11. Stedman Jones, *Outcast London*, p. 217.

12. Offer, *Property and Politics*, p. 239.

13. Report of the Real Property Commissioners, p. 14 (cited in A. W. B Simpson, *An Introduction to the History of Land Law*, Oxford University Press (1961), p. 162).

14. Stedman Jones, *Outcast London*, pp. 201–2.

15. Frank Paish, 'The Economics of Rent Restriction', in Hayek et al., eds, *Verdict on Rent Control: Essays on the Economic Consequences of Political Action to Restrict Rents in Five Countries* (London: Institute of Economic Affairs, 1972), p. 50.

16. Malcolm Allan, 'A Future in Private Renting?', *Built Environment Quarterly* 2: 4 (1976), pp. 298–304.

17. *Hansard*, House of Commons, 23 January 1975, HC Debs vol. 883, col. 2,081.

18. Adah Kaye, Marjorie Mayo and Mike Thompson, 'Inner London's Housing Crisis', in John Cowley, Adah Kaye, Marjorie Mayo and Mike Thompson, *Community or Class Struggle?* (London: Stage 1, 1977), p. 158.

19. Ibid., p. 158.

20. *The Right Approach*, Conservative Party policy statement, 4 October 1976 – available at margaretthatcher.org.

21. John Enoch Powell, 'White Paper on Housing Policy: Memorandum of the Minister of Health', 14 May 1963.

22. Peter Apps, 'Housing Supply "Overshadowed" Fire Safety Despite Multiple Warnings Before Grenfell, Barwell Accepts', *Inside Housing*, 5 April 2022.

23. R. Patten, B. Cassidy, A. Hinton, R. Schindler, A. Tate and F. Taylor, *Eclipse of the Private Landlord*, Conservative Political Centre for the Junior Carlton Club (1974), pp. 13–14.

24. John Boughton, *Municipal Dreams: The Rise and Fall of Council Housing* (London: Verso, 2019), pp. 238–42.

25. Danny Dorling, *All That Is Solid: How the Great Housing Disaster Defines Our Times, and What We Can Do About It* (London: Penguin, 2015), pp. 158–9.

26. Jim Connolly and James Stewart, 'Private Renters Stuck in Dangerous Homes "Failed" by Councils', BBC News, 10 November 2022.

3. The Making of the English Landlord Class

1. John Burnett, *A Social History of Housing 1815–1970* (Exeter: David & Charles, 1978), p. 174.

2. Nigel Lewis, 'Government Reveals Where All the Landlords Live in the UK', *Negotiator*, 29 July 2021; written ministerial answer UIN HL20 80 (Lord Agnew of Oulton), 27 July 2021 – at parliament.uk; HM Revenue and Customs, 'Official Statistics: Property Rental Income Statistics: 2022', 27 October 2022.

3. Richard Ronald and Justin Kadi, 'The Revival of Private Landlords in Britain's Post-Homeownership Society', *New Political Economy* 23: 6 (2018).

4. Theodor Adorno, 'Sexual Taboos and Law Today' (1963), transl. Henry W. Pickford, in Adorno, *Critical Models: Interventions and Catchwords* (New York: Columbia University Press, 1998), p. 71.

5. Friedrich Engels, *The Housing Question* (Moscow: Progress Publishers, 1970), pp. 29–30.

6. Acts of the Privy Council of England (Colonial Series), Vol. IV (1745–66), p. 591 (26 March 1764), referred to in David Madden and Peter Marcuse, *In Defense of Housing: The Politics of Crisis* (London: Verso, 2016), p. 95.

7. David Harvey, *The Limits to Capital* (London: Verso, 2018), p. 360.

8. See, for example, Simon Clarke and Norman Ginsburg, 'The Political Economy of Housing', Political Economy of Housing Group (1974) – available at warwick.ac.uk.

9. Hamptons Estate Agents, 'Annual Rent Bill to hit £63bn', July 2022, at hamptons.co.uk.

10. *English Private Landlord Survey 2021: Main Report*, Department for Levelling Up, Housing and Communities, May 2022, p. 10; Joe Beswick, Georgia Alexandri, Michael Byrne, Sònia Vives-Miró, Desiree Fields, Stuart Hodkinson and Michael Janoschka, 'Speculating on London's Housing Future', *City* 20: 2 (2016), p. 330.

11. Sir Edward Milner Holland QC, *Report of the Committee on Housing in Greater London*, HM Stationery Office (Cmd. 2605), March 1965 – available at wellcomecollection.org; *Hansard*, House of Lords, 29 March 1965 (HL Debs vol. 264, col. 867).

12. Owen Hatherley, *Red Metropolis: Socialism and the Government of London* (London: Repeater, 2020), p. 69.

13. Milner Holland, *Report of the Committee on Housing in Greater London*, p. 39.

14. Joel Barnett, *The Politics of Legislation: The Rent Act 1957* (London: Weidenfeld & Nicolson, 1969), pp. 17, 203–5.

15. Ibid., p. 195, citing Walter Block, *Developments in Rent Control Between 1915 and 1955* (London, 1955), and Conservative Party Research Department pamphlets.

16. Milner Holland, *Report of the Committee on Housing in Greater London*, pp. 39, 44; John Davis, 'Rents and Race in 1960s London: New Light on Rachmanism', *Twentieth Century British History* 12: 1 (2001), p. 75.

17. The 'property boom channelling wealth into the hands of individuals' described by Oliver Marriott (see Chapter 1).

18. See, for example, Manuel Aalbers and Brett Christophers, 'Centring Housing in Political Economy', *Housing, Theory and Society* 31: 4 (2014), p. 378; Raquel Rolnik, *Urban Warfare: Housing Under the Empire of Finance* (London: Verso, 2019), p. 31.

19. *Hansard*, House of Commons, 22 July 1963 (HC Debs vol. 681, col. 1068).

20. Kathleen Scanlon and Christine M. E. Whitehead, *The Profile of UK Private Landlords* (London: Council of Mortgage Lenders, 2016), p. 9.

21. Mark Smulian, 'Housing Benefit Cap Will Force Down Private Rents, Says Freud', *Public Finance*, 3 November 2010.

22. Aalbers and Christophers, 'Centring Housing in Political Economy', p. 378.

23. Madden and Marcuse, *In Defense of Housing*, p. 98.

24. *Hansard*, House of Commons, 13 December 1993 (HC Debs vol. 273, col. 221).

25. Resolution Foundation, *Stagnation Nation: Navigating a Route to a Fairer and More Prosperous Britain*, interim report July 2022, p. 13.

26. Office for National Statistics, *UK House Price Index: June 2021*, statistical bulletin, p. 4.

27. Farhad Farnood and Colin Jones, 'The Changing Image of the UK Private Landlord with the Buy to Let Revolution', *Journal of Housing and the Built Environment* 38: 1 (2022).

28. 'TV's Top Property Shows', *Guardian*, 21 February 2003.

29. Ministry of Housing, Communities and Local Government, *Banning Order Offences under the Housing and Planning Act 2016: Guidance for Local Housing Authorities*, April 2018.

30. Rajeev Syal, 'Jeremy Corbyn Vows to Take On Exploitative Landlords if Elected PM', *Guardian*, 24 November 2019.

31. *Hansard*, House of Commons, 22 July 1963 (HC Debs vol. 681, col. 1060).

32. Liam Reynolds, *Research Report: Survey of Private Landlords*, Shelter, February 2016, p. 3.

33. *McDonald v McDonald* [2017] AC 273, SC.

34. *Drane v Evangelou* [1978] 1 WLR 455, CA.

35. Victor Hugo, *Les Misérables* (Paris: Pocket, 2013), p. 104: 'Il y a dans notre civilisation des heures redoubtables; ce sont les moments où la pénalité pronounce un naufrage.'

36. Adam Blanden, 'Safe as Houses? Can the Tories Keep Their Electoral Coalition Together?', *New Socialist*, 30 March 2022.

37. See, for example, Costas Lapavitsas, *The Left Case Against the EU* (Cambridge: Polity, 2019), Chapter 3, which argues that part of Germany's economic success has been founded on a deliberate avoidance of mortgage finance and associated household debt.

38. Alan Smart, *Making Room: Squatter Clearance in Hong Kong*, University of Hong Kong, Centre for Asian Studies Occasional Papers, No. 102 (1992), discussed in Mike Davis, *Planet of Slums* (London: Verso, 2017), p. 63.

39. Francesca T. C. Manning, 'Landownership and Class', *Historical Materialism Podcast*, 2 February 2023.

40. Evidence of Charles Richard Weld, Esq., *Minutes of Evidence Taken Before the Select Committee on Health of Towns* (1840), p. 68 – available at wellcomecollection.org.

41. Perri 6, 'Back to the 1850s: A Free Market in Housing, *Socialist Lawyer* 3 (Autumn 1987), pp. 17–18. The editorial board of this edition included a young Keir Starmer.

42. David Harvey, *The Limits to Capital* (London: Verso, 2018), p. 348.

4. Solving Things Ourselves

1. Giles Peaker, 'Southwark Gatekeeping: All of the Wrong', *Nearly Legal: Housing Law News and Comment*, 22 February 2015, at nearlylegal.co.uk.

2. Simon Clarke and Norman Ginsburg, 'The Political Economy of Housing', Political Economy of Housing Group (1974), p. 8 – available at warwick.ac.uk.

3. A. Sivanandan, *Catching History on the Wing*, speech at Institute of Race Relations' fiftieth anniversary conference and celebration, 1 November 2008 (available at irr.org.uk).

4. William Gallacher, *Revolt on the Clyde* (London: Lawrence & Wishart, 2017), p. 57.

5. Ibid. p. 58.

6. Ibid.

7. David Watkinson, 'Abolishing Section 21: Restricting Renting or Technocratic Tinkering?', lecture to the Haldane Society of Socialist Lawyers, 9 October 2019 – available at youtube.com.

8. David Renton, *Against the Law: Why Justice Requires Fewer Laws and a Smaller State* (London: Repeater, 2022), p. 41.

9. Quoted in Past Tense, 'Rent Strike Now? Inspiration from the 1915 Glasgow Rent Strike', 27 April 2020, at pasttenseblog.wordpress.com.

10. Clarke and Ginsburg, 'Political Economy of Housing', p. 8.

11. Speech at Buckingham Palace to representatives of local authorities and societies, *The Times*, 12 April 1919 – cited in John Burnett, *A Social History of Housing 1815– 1970* (Exeter: David & Charles, 1978), p. 215.

12. Avner Offer, *Property and Politics 1870–1914: Landownership, Law, Ideology and Urban Development in England* (Cambridge: CUP, 1981), p. 141.

13. Gareth Stedman Jones, *Outcast London: A Study in the Relationship Between Classes in Victorian Society* (London: Verso, 2013), p. 224.

14. Plutarch, *The Life of Tiberius Gracchus*, 9.3, transl. Michael Engelhardt-Sprack (personal communication to the author together with the epigram to the conclusion [see p.192]).

15. Race Today Collective, 'East End Housing Campaign', *Race Today*, December 1975 – cited in Paul Field, Robin Bunce, Leila Hassan and Margaret Peacock, eds, *Here to Stay, Here to Fight: A 'Race Today' Anthology* (London: Pluto, 2019), p. 117.

16. Clarke and Ginsburg, 'Political Economy of Housing', p. 8.

17. Ibid., p. 9.

18. Ellen Meiksins Wood, *The Origin of Capitalism: A Longer View* (London: Verso, 2002), p. 94. See also Christopher Hill, *The World Turned Upside-Down* (London: Penguin, 1991), pp. 378–84.

19. Henri Lefebvre, *Le Droit à la Ville, suivi de Espace et Politique* (Paris: Anthropos, 1968).

20. Mike Davis, 'Who Will Build the Ark?', *New Left Review*, vol. 61 (Jan/Feb 2010).

21. 'Tenants in Revolt' (1939) – available at player.bfi.org.uk.

22. Quoted in Past Tense, 'Rent Strike Now?'.

23. *Hansard*, House of Commons, 22 June 1939 (HC Debs vol. 348, col. 2440).

24. Quintin Bradley, 'Leeds Rent Strike 1914', *Critical Place*, at criticalplace.org.uk; Past Tense, 'Rent Strike Now?'.

25. *Camden Nominees v. Forcey & Slack* [1940] Ch 352; *St Pancras: Homes or Slums?*, Communist Party of Great Britain (St Pancras Branch) (1945), p. 6.

26. Phil Piratin, *Our Flag Stays Red* (London: Lawrence & Wishart, 2006), p. 40.

27. Ibid., p. 45.

28. John Cowley, Adah Kaye, Marjorie Mayo and Mike Thompson, *Community or Class Struggle?* (London: Stage 1, 1977), p. 176. My thanks to the authors of the excellent Southwark Notes blog (southwarknotes.wordpress.com) for tracking down this fascinating source.

29. Sienna Rogers, '"Cancel the Rent" Policy Would Be "un-Labour", Says Debbonaire', *Labour List*, 14 May 2020.

30. See Chapter 7.

31. Mike Davis, *Old Gods, New Enigmas* (London: Verso, 2020), p. 48.

5. Illegitimate Concerns

1. Emily Twinch, 'Prince Philip's Patel Quip "Not a Gaffe", Says Chief Executive', *Inside Housing*, 27 October 2009, at insidehousing.co.uk.

2. House of Commons Women and Equalities Committee, *Unequal Impact? Coronavirus and BAME People*, Third Report of Session 2019–21, 15 December 2020, pp. 37–41.

3. Ruth Wilson Gilmore, *Golden Gulag: Prisons, Surplus, Crisis, and Opposition in Globalizing California* (Stanford, CA: University of California Press, 2006), p. 28. For a discussion of Gilmore's definition in the British sociolegal context, see Nadine El-Enany, *(B)ordering Britain: Law, Race and Empire* (Manchester: Manchester University Press, 2020), pp. 24–6; Michael Richmond and Alex Charnley, *Fractured: Race, Class, Gender and the Hatred of Identity Politics* (London: Pluto, 2022).

4. Gargi Bhattacharyya, *Rethinking Racial Capitalism: Questions of Reproduction and Survival* (Lanham, MD: Rowman & Littlefield, 2018), Introduction, Thesis 1.

5. El-Enany, *(B)ordering Britain*, p. 17.

6. Ibid. p. ix.

7. Quoted in John Parton, *Some Account of the Hospital and Parish of St Giles in the Fields, Middlesex* (London: Luke Hansard & Sons, 1821).

8. *R (Joint Council for the Welfare of Immigrants) v Secretary of State for the Home Department* [2021] 1 WLR 1151, CA.

9. Bhattacharyya, *Rethinking Racial Capitalism*, p. 102.

10. Lucy Pasha-Robinson and Matt Murphy, 'Kensington Residents Express Dismay at Grenfell Fire Victims' Nearby Rehousing: "I Don't Want Them Here"', *Independent*, 23 June 2017.

11. Alistair Cartwright, 'Rented Worlds: Bedsits, Boarding Houses and Multiple Occupancy Homes in Postwar London, 1945–1963', PhD thesis, Birkbeck, University of London (2020), p. 264.

12. Sir Edward Milner Holland QC et al., *Report of the Committee on Housing in Greater London*, HM Stationery Office (Cmd. 2605), March 1965, pp. 189, 192 – available at wellcomecollection.org.

13. Ibid., p. 190.

14. Cartwright, 'Rented Worlds', p. 271.

15. John Davis, 'Rents and Race in 1960s London: New Light on Rachmanism', *Twentieth Century British History* 12: 1 (2001).

16. *Hansard*, House of Commons, 22 July 1963 (HC Debs vol. 681, col.1083).

17. Davis, 'Rents and Race in 1960s London', p. 82.

18. 'Ethnicity Facts and Figures: Home Ownership', at tinyurl.com/yvvzdxdj.

19. Adam Almeida, *Pushed to the Margins: A Quantitative Analysis of Gentrification in London in the 2010s*, Runnymede and CLASS (June 2021).

20. *Hansard*, House of Commons, 18 February 1903 (HC Debs vol. 118, col. 197).

21. *Hansard*, House of Commons, 1 November 1909 (HC Debs vol. 12, col. 1353).

22. Steve Cohen, *No One Is Illegal: Asylum and Immigration Control Past and Present* (Stoke-on-Trent: Trentham, 2003), p. 97, citing criticisms made by the Board of Deputies of British Jews reported in the *Jewish Chronicle* (together with *Chronicle*'s own editorial), 20 March 1925.

23. Sam Wetherell, *Foundations: How the Built Environment Made Twentieth-Century Britain* (Princeton, NJ: Princeton University Press, 2020), p. 116.

24. John Boughton, *Municipal Dreams: The Rise and Fall of Council Housing* (London: Verso, 2019), p. 213.

25. Wetherell, *Foundations*, p. 100.

26. Paul Field, Robin Bunce, Leila Hassan and Margaret Peacock, eds, *Here To Stay, Here To Fight: A 'Race Today' Anthology* (London: Pluto, 2019), p. 121.

27. Ibid., p. 116.

28. Peter Apps, 'The Grenfell Tower Fire Was Part of Britain's Colonial Legacy', *Tribune*, 21 September 2022.

29. ARK Consultancy, *Croydon Council: Independent Investigation*, May 2021 – available at croydon.gov.uk.

30. Giles Peaker, 'An Avoidable Death', *Nearly Legal: Housing Law News and Comment*, 15 November 2022, at nearlylegal.co.uk; Peter Apps on Twitter: 'Shocked to hear a source say that when landlords talk about "ritual bathing" in the context of damp, it's a reference to Muslim families washing hands, face and feet before prayers. If that is the case, it's about the most ignorant, xenophobic and disguting [*sic*] thing I've ever heard', 8 February 2023, at tinyurl.com/2p9ejmjh.

31. Richmond and Charnley, *Fractured*, pp. 159–61.

32. Patrick Collinson, 'Landlord's Ban on "Coloured" Tenants Is Unlawful, Court Rules', *Guardian*, 8 November 2017.

33. *Ashford Borough Council v Fergus Wilson* [2021] EWHC 2542 (QB).

34. G. Bramley, S. Fitzpatrick, J. McIntyre and S. Johnson, *Homelessness Amongst Black and Minoritised Ethnic Communities in the UK: A Statistical Report on the State of the Nation* (Edinburgh: Heriot-Watt University, 2022).

35. Jacqui Banerjee, Madeleine Green and Kath Scanlon, *Right to Rent Scheme: Phase Two Evaluation*, Home Office, 9 February 2023, §3.1.2.

36. 'Ethnicity Facts and Figures: State Support', at tinyurl.com/4xn7y78r.

37. Kevin Gulliver, *Racial Discrimination in UK Housing Has a Long History and Deep Roots*, LSE British Politics and Policy blog, 12 October 2017, at blogs.lse.ac.uk.

38. Lucie Heath, 'Racial Inequality "Hard-Wired into Housing System" as UK Rent Soars, Polling Reveals', *i News*, 9 October 2022.

39. Vicky Spratt, *Tenants: The People on the Frontline of Britain's Housing Emergency* (London: Profile, 2022), p. 52.

40. Jack Lewis, 'British Capitalism, the Welfare State and the First Radicalisation of State Employees', in John Cowley, Adah Kaye, Marjorie Mayo and Mike Thompson, *Community or Class Struggle?* (London: Stage 1, 1977), p. 122.

41. David Madden and Peter Marcuse, *In Defense of Housing: The Politics of Crisis* (London: Verso, 2016), p. 108.

42. Field et al., *Here to Stay, Here to Fight*, pp. 119–20.

43. Richard Vinen, *Second City: Birmingham and the Forging of Modern Britain* (London: Penguin, 2022), pp. 248–9.

44. Tice Cin, 'Loopholes', *Granta*, 7 March 2023.

45. Owen Hatherley, 'The Making and Unmaking of the Council Estate', *Tribune*, 12 November 2020.

46. Nick Bano, 'Justice for Grenfell – What Does It Mean?' *The Justice Gap*, 23 June 2017, at thejusticegap.com.

47. Isabella Mulholland, *Abused Twice*, report by the Public Interest Law Centre, September 2022.

48. George Head, *Giant London: The Evolution of a Great City in Size and Value* (London: Surveyors' Institution, 1909), p. 336 – cited in Avner Offer, *Property and Politics 1870–1914: Landownership, Law, Ideology and Urban Development in England* (Cambridge: CUP, 1981), p. 309.

6. Everything Everywhere All at Once

1. Isaac Rose, *Rentier City: Manchester and the Making of the Neoliberal Metropolis* (London: Repeater, 2024).

2. Rachel Hall, 'One in Four Londoners in Temporary Housing Outside Their Local Area', *Guardian*, 2 June 2021; Keith Cooper and Matthew Weaver, 'Hundreds More Homeless Families Rehoused Outside Local Area in England', *Guardian*, 24 October 2022.

3. Tom Hazeldine, *The Northern Question: A History of a Divided Country* (London: Verso, 2022), p. 222.

4. Simon Jenkins, *Landlords to London: The Story of a Capital and Its Growth* (London: Constable, 1975), p. 185.

5. HM Government, *Levelling Up the United Kingdom: Executive Summary*, February 2022, p. 7 – at gov.uk.

6. David Harvey, *The Limits to Capital* (London: Verso, 2018), p. 338.

7. Hazeldine, *Northern Question*, p. 186.

8. Doreen Massey, *World City* (Cambridge: Polity, 2013), pp. 99–100.

9. For more on Wates, see Chapter 7. 'Government Unveils New Levelling Up Plan to Close the North–South Divide', *PBC Today*, 3 February 2022.

10. Antonia Cundy, 'Manchester's Property Prices Keep Moving On Up', *Financial Times*, 7 April 2021.

11. Owen Hatherley, *A Guide to the New Ruins of Great Britain* (London: Verso, 2011), p. 115.

12. Owen Hatherley, 'Manchester's New Ruins, Ten Years On', *Meteor*, 7 June 2020.

13. John Burnett, *A Social History of Housing 1815–1970* (Exeter: David & Charles, 1978), p. 146.

14. 'Citylights – Citylets Quarterly Report – Q1 2022', *Citylets: Home of Scottish Letting*, at citylets.co.uk.

15. Tom Blackburn, 'Telling the Tale of England's North Country Blues', *Jacobin*, 17 October 2020.

16. Lily Gordon Brown, 'A New Hope? How the Liverpool City Region Is Pioneering New Pathways in Community Land Ownership', Greater Manchester Housing Action blog, 30 November 2020, at gmhousingaction.com.

17. Christine Toner, 'The Credit Crunch 10 Years On: How Liverpool's Housing Market Has Changed', *YM Liverpool*, 11 August 2017.

18. Press release: 'Deputy Prime Minister Plans to Bring Empty Buildings Back to Life in the North', Deputy Prime Minister's Office, 26 November 2014.

19. 'Bradford Shamed in League of Empty Homes Hotspots', *Yorkshire Post*, 25 May 2016.

20. Hazeldine, *Northern Question*, p. 99.

21. David Adler and Ben Ansell 'Housing and Populism', *West European Politics* 43: 2 (2020).

22. Massey, *World City*, p. 98.

23. Office for National Statistics, *Housing Affordability in England and Wales: 2021*, 23 March 2022.

24. Land Registry data featured in Edwin Heathcote, 'Could Co-Living Ease the UK Countryside's Housing Crisis?', *Financial Times*, 5 August 2022; ONS *Housing Affordability in England and Wales: 2021*.

25. Simon Clarke and Norman Ginsburg, 'The Political Economy of Housing', Political Economy of Housing Group (1974), p. 5 – available at warwick.ac.uk.

26. Adam Blanden, 'Safe as Houses? Can the Tories Keep Their Electoral Coalition Together?', *New Socialist*, 30 March 2022.

27. Taj Ali, 'The Staycation Crisis', *Tribune*, 27 August 2021.

7. The House Always Wins?

1. Danny Dorling, *All That Is Solid: How the Great Housing Disaster Defines Our Times, and What We Can Do About It* (London: Penguin, 2015), pp. 171–3.

2. 'Yield Map: Best London Rental Yields 2022 & 2023', at portico.com.

3. Council of Mortgage Lenders, *The Profile of UK Private Landlords*, December 2016, p. 48.

4. Nick Bano, 'The Making of the Microflat', *Tribune*, 16 November 2021.

5. Chris Flood, Josephine Cumbo, George Hammond and Adrienne Klasa, 'UK Property Funds Limit Withdrawals as Pension Funds Shift Assets', *Financial Times*, 3 October 2022.

6. *First Report of Her Majesty's Commissioners for Inquiring into the Housing of the Working Classes* (1889), p. 31 – available at wellcomecollection.org.

7. Mike Davis, *Planet of Slums* (London: Verso, 2017), p. 83.

8. Mike Davis, *Late Victorian Holocausts: El Niño Famines and the Making of the Third World* (London: Verso, 2017), Chapter 5.

9. See Chapter 5.

10. Cited in Avner Offer, *Property and Politics 1870–1914: Landownership, Law, Ideology and Urban Development in England* (Cambridge: CUP, 1981), p. 282.

11. Sarah Butler, 'More than One in Eight UK Households Fear They Have No Way of Making More Cuts', *Guardian*, 1 August 2022.

12. Sam Wetherell, *Foundations: How the Built Environment Made Twentieth-Century Britain* (Princeton, NJ: Princeton University Press, 2020), p. 89.

13. See Chapters 1 and 3.

14. Melissa Lawford, 'Half a Million Landlords to Be Hit by Soaring Costs as Fixed Rate Mortgages Expire', *Telegraph*, 14 December 2022.

15. See Chapter 1.

16. Joe Beswick, Georgia Alexandri, Michael Byrne, Sònia Vives-Miró, Desiree Fields, Stuart Hodkinson and Michael Janoschka, 'Speculating on London's Housing Future', *City* 20: 2 (2016), p. 331.

17. News release, 'Bank of England Widens Gilt Purchase Operations to Include Index-Linked Gilts', 11 October 2022 – available at bankofengland.co.uk.

18. Tommy Stubbington and Chris Giles, 'Investors believe BoE's QE Programme Is Designed to Finance UK Deficit, *Financial Times*, 5 January 2021.

19. Patrick Jenkins, 'The Triple Whammy for Office Real Estate', *Financial Times*, 1 August 2022.

20. Karl Marx, *Capital, Volume III* (Harmondsworth: Penguin, 1991), p. 909. My emphasis. See also *Capital, Volume II* (Harmondsworth: Penguin, 1992), pp. 311–12, to which Marx cross-refers. Modern-day developers candidly admit this fact: see Sophie K. Rosa, *Radical Intimacy* (London: Pluto, 2023) p. 114, quoting a director of Ballymore: 'Yes, ultimately, we have the sinister goal of increasing property prices, but it doesn't mean we don't care about culture!' It is worth noting that Marx's naive belief that speculative building was a relatively recent Victorian development – which he based on the anecdotal and nostalgic account of a house builder giving evidence to a parliamentary committee – stands in contrast to the argument of Chapter 2 of this book, as well as a great deal of later writing on the subject.

21. David Harvey, *The Limits to Capital* (London: Verso, 2018), pp. 347–9.

22. Ibid. p. 349.

23. Joe Bilsborough, 'Rentier Island', *Tribune*, 14 March 2021.

24. Office for National Statistics, *National Balance Sheet Estimates for the UK: 2021*, 2 November 2021, section 3.

25. Phyllis Deane and W. A. Cole, *British Economic Growth 1688–1959: Trends and Structure* (Cambridge: CUP, 1962), cited in Offer, *Property and Politics*, p. 6.

26. Matthew Watson, 'House Price Keynesianism and the Contradictions of the Modern Investor Subject', *Housing Studies* 25: 3 (2010), pp. 413–26; Colin Crouch, *The Strange Non-Death of Neoliberalism* (Cambridge: Polity, 2011).

27. William Letwin, *The Origins of Scientific Economics* (London: Routledge, 2010), pp. 53–4.

28. Thomas Macaulay, *The History of England from the Accession of James the Second* (1848), vol. 4, Chapter XX.

29. Hilary Osborne, 'Millennials Will Spend £53,000 on Rent Before Age of 30, Think-tank Says', *Guardian*, 16 July 2016.

30. John Lewis and Fergus Cumming, 'Houses Are Assets Not Goods: What the Difference Between Bulbs and Flowers Tells Us About the Housing Market', Bank of England staff's 'Bank Underground' blog, 5 September 2019, at bankunderground.co.uk.

31. House of Commons Housing Communities and Local Government Committee, *Building More Social Housing: Third Report of Session 2019–21*, 20 July 2020, p. 19.

32. *Camfield v Uyiekpen* [2022] UKUT 234 (LC).

33. 'Wall St Titans Lay Claim to Affordable Housing', *Financial Times*, 28 August–29 August 2021; 'RiseBoro and Blackstone Announce Agreement to Preserve Affordable Housing', Affordable Housing Finance, 6 July 2022, at housingfinance.com.

34. Richard Goulding, Adam Leaver and Jonathan Silver, *Manchester Off-Shored: A Public Interest Report on the Manchester Life Partnership between Manchester City Council and the Abu Dhabi United Group*, Centripedal Cities (available at sheffield.ac.uk).

35. Havering Council, 'Havering & Wates Joint Venture Business Plan Update – 2021 /22' – available at democracy.havering.gov.uk.

36. Savills, *Spotlight: East London Corridor Development*, 19 April 2021, at savills.co.uk.

37. Owen Hatherley, 'The Government of London', *New Left Review* II/122 (March–April 2021).

38. *Kerslake Review of Affordable Housing in Lambeth*, November 2022 (available at lambeth.gov.uk).

Conclusion

1. Afiq Fitri, 'The UK Now Spends More on Housing Benefit than on Most Government Departments', *New Statesman*, 14 November 2022.

2. See, for example, Frank Paish, 'The Economics of Rent Restriction', in F. A. Hayek et al., eds, *Verdict on Rent Control: Essays on the Economic Consequences of Political Action to Restrict Rents in Five Countries* (London: Institute of Economic Affairs, 1972), p. 51.

3. Karl Marx and Friedrich Engels, *Manifesto of the Communist Party* (London: Lawrence & Wishart (Little Lenin Library series, 1941), p. 28. My emphasis.

4. Karl Marx, 'The Nationalisation of Land', paper read at the Manchester Section of the International Working Men's Association 1872 – available at marxists.org.

5. Simon Clarke and Norman Ginsburg, 'The Political Economy of Housing', University of Warwick, Political Economy of Housing Group (1974), p. 17 – available at warwick.ac.uk.

6. Milner Holland et al., *Report of the Committee on Housing in Greater London*, HM Stationery Office (Cmd. 2605), March 1965, p. 5 – available at wellcomecollection.org.

7. Gareth Stedman Jones, *Outcast London: A Study in the Relationship Between Classes in Victorian Society* (London: Verso, 2013), p. 186.

8. *Hansard*, House of Commons 30 January 1947 (HC Debs vol. 432, col. 1230–1232).

9. Jeffrey. A. Nedoroskik, *The City of the Dead: History of Cairo's Cemetery Communities* (Bergin & Garvey, 1997), quoted in Mike Davis, *Planet of Slums* (London: Verso, 2017), pp. 85–6.

Index